About the author

Roger Mavity founded his own advertising agency, Mavity Gilmore Jaume, in 1981 and went on to win the advertising for Honda, Minolta, Burberry, Nestlé, Hotpoint and more. He sold the business to a French group and left in 1991.

He then joined Granada Group, first as Chief Executive of the Leisure Division and then as Chief Executive of the Technology Division. At Granada he masterminded the company's successful pitch to the city to buy Forte Group – still the biggest hostile takeover bid in British commercial history, as well as perhaps the most bitter. He then became Chairman of Citigate, one of the UK's most respected financial PR companies, before becoming Chief Executive of the Conran Group in 2006.

He was Chief Executive of Conran for seven years, leaving in 2013 to concentrate on writing and photography. As an art photographer, his work has been exhibited in London, Paris, Brussels, Ghent and Amsterdam. He is also a trustee of The Photographers' Gallery.

This is his second book. His first, *Life's a Pitch*, was co-authored with Stephen Bayley, and went on to become an international bestseller.

THE RULE BREAK ER'S
BOOK OF BUSINESS

ROGER MAVITY

piatkus

PIATKUS

First published in Great Britain in 2013 by Piatkus

Copyright © Roger Mavity 2013

The moral right of the author has been asserted.

A CIP catalogue record for this book
is available from the British Library.

ISBN 978-0-7499-5907-4

Typeset in Minion by M Rules
Printed and bound in Great Britain by
Clays Ltd, St Ives plc

Papers used by Piatkus are from well-managed forests
and other responsible sources.

MIX
Paper from
responsible sources
FSC® C104740

Piatkus
An imprint of
Little, Brown Book Group
100 Victoria Embankment
London EC4Y 0DY

An Hachette UK Company
www.hachette.co.uk

www.piatkus.co.uk

Anti-dedication

It's traditional for authors to dedicate a book to someone they admire, someone who has inspired them. My last book, which I wrote with Stephen Bayley, was dedicated to Machiavelli, whose splendid ruthlessness certainly inspired us.

But this time, in the spirit of rebellion, I'd like to 'anti-dedicate' my book: to identify someone I abhor, someone who represents the antithesis of what I believe. So I am anti-dedicating this book to James McKinsey, the father of modern management consultancy, and the man who did more than anyone to propagate the notion that business success depends on arid numerical analysis rather than drive, vision, passion and ideas.

The Rule Breaker's Book of Business describes how to achieve business success by ignoring conventional wisdom, instead of being trapped by it. It extols the virtues of passion rather than process, of the lateral rather than the logical.

At its heart lies the simple credo that you won't get a different result if you aren't brave enough to follow a different direction.

Contents List

HOW TO DEAL WITH YOURSELF

Foreword
by Stephen Bayley

I am not saying that Roger Mavity is the new Machiavelli. There is still mileage in the old one and, besides, Roger has a more developed sense of humour. What I am saying is that Rog (as his friends know him) has spent a lifetime alternately in the service of tyrants or disciplining willful creative types, arguing with supine advisers, haggling with banks, pitching to clients, supporting tearful staff, jollying-up consultancies, head-banging journalists and, generally, keeping whatever vessel he happens to be aboard at the time afloat and on the right course to a cheerful destination. '*Si guarda al fine*', as Machiavelli once said: 'Always have the desired result in sight'. The culmination of all this experience – some clement, some tempestuous, all of it interesting – is this clever book in front of you.

Unlike Machiavelli himself, Rog has never, at least so far as I know, been exiled – although some may have wished it. But his huge catalogue of experience in and out of ad agencies, at the front of takeover battles, in design and PR consultancies during the most clamorous period in London's epic business history, has afforded him as many insights into the variety of human natures as Machiavelli won at the Medici court. Rog is not often surprised by sudden events. He has started businesses, bought businesses, sold businesses and folded them. He has usually been promoted. He has sometimes been sacked. He always comes back. He is never lost for words. Those close to him have never heard him say 'I don't know'. He has possibly not seen it all, but he has seen a great deal of it. He has earned what the French call *le droit du donner les lecons* – the right to teach.

But in writing this book Rog is not offering an orthodox account of how to survive and prosper in business. Instead, it is an unorthodox one. Of course, Machiavelli knew the importance of disturbing the status quo. And I am certain Rog was inspired by Machiavelli's belief that 'obstacle and opportunity are the same thing'. But this is taken further here. Rog knows and teaches that it is important to tolerate mistakes. A mistake is not a misfortune: it's a happy discovery of how not to do something. As Churchill said, the route to success is largely comprised of the ability to go from one failure to the next with no loss of enthusiasm. Or, as Junior Walker and The All Stars sang: 'Keep on keeping on'. What this book tells us is, be certain to know the result you are after, but understand and enjoy (and, dear reader, manipulate) the process on the way.

But you should show, not merely tell: this is an instructive, inspiring, humorous and occasionally touching account of one successful businessman's ups, downs, ins and outs. It's an overview and a sideswipe, a periscope-depth survey by a fearless navigator in the choppy waters of creative commerce. Or maybe I mean commercial creativity. Only the dullest reader could not learn from it. But it would count for nothing so much if Rog himself had not visited The Other Side. After more down-and-dirty experience as a suit in senior management than few would wish to replicate, Rog decided to become a writer and a photographer. He became the first with absolute professionalism, and he became the second with huge style. He made mistakes, but he bashed on. It was all a success.

In all of this, there's an important consistency. It's rather as the old buffer of an academic once declared: 'I always say the same thing, but I never repeat myself.' There's a clear and certain voice here which I know and like. And I feel a bit wistful writing this as Rog's first book was a collaboration with me. I wouldn't say we were Lennon and McCartney, still less Jobs and Ive. Maybe more Gilbert and George, or Morecambe and Wise. He asked me to collaborate on this one, but I had to refuse since I know nothing about business. But over the years I have learnt a huge amount from Rog and recognise what I have learnt in the pages that follow. It's a fortunate reader who buys this executive summary of an executive's intellectual adventures.

Never mind if there's an inherent paradox: understand these rules – then you must break them. If you read this book and then start thinking differently, an important point will have been made.

Already in trouble, and we haven't even begun yet ...

The simple aim of this book is to take a lifetime of experiences in business – some good, some bad – and to turn those experiences into a route map through the hostile jungle we call the world of work.

In that jungle you'll meet all kinds of people – journalists, lawyers, accountants, shareholders, customers, employees, employers. Some of them will be men, some will be women. If, every time I refer to someone I say 'he, or she, as the case may be' it will make for a style which is repetitive and awkward for you to read. It will, come to think about it, also be repetitive and awkward for me to write. So I'm just going to refer to this imaginary person as 'he'.

Believe me, that's not because I'm some mad, reactionary anti-feminist, it's just because I'd like the book to read like a book you might actually enjoy rather than like a legal document.

So, I'm already in trouble with committed feminists, and we haven't even begun yet ...

Is your work fun? Could it be? Should it be?

At a time of intensifying global economic anxiety, worrying about whether your work is *fun* may seem a little frivolous. After all, most people with a job are pleased just to have one.

Yet work occupies a huge share of our waking lives, pays for our food and a roof over our head, and absorbs more than its fair share of our emotional energy.

Given that, wouldn't we want work to be a source of joy as well as a source of income?

Above all, don't we recognise that when we enjoy work we do it better?

When I say that work should be fun, I don't mean fun in the sense of drinking too much free Prosecco at the office party. I mean fun in a deeper sense: that work should be a source of stimulus, of pride, of the self-belief that comes when we've faced up to a task we're a bit frightened of and pulled it off successfully.

This book is devoted to the simple – but vital – ideal that success at work matters to us, and is much more likely to be achieved if we are happy and confident in what we do.

But this book also believes that fun, and success, at work doesn't come from slavishly following the rules. On the contrary, it's only by ignoring the conventional wisdom, by breaking a few rules, by daring to use different means, that we have a chance of achieving different ends.

Unsurprisingly, conventional wisdom tends to produce conventional results. If we are going to create something remarkable, we need a new kind of mindset: we need to stand outside the usual way of doing things and attack problems with a more original vision. That's what this book is about.

To help find that new mindset, we now need to indulge ourselves with a quick moment of ornithology . . .

Left brains, right brains, and the relevance of ornithology to success at work

Neuroscientists believe that the left side of the brain is more concerned with analysis and the right side is more concerned with creativity. Of course, we all need both types of thinking, but getting the right balance between the two is crucial.

Analysis is preoccupied with what's there (you can't analyse something which doesn't exist) while creativity is more interested in what *could* be there. As a consequence, left-brain thought is not only analytical, it's also detail-sensitive. People who analyse want to get into the small print, to understand all the detail. Right-brain thought is much more 'big picture': because it's about possibilities and ideas, it's more concerned with vision than detail.

If I wanted to commission a great painting to hang in my home, I'd want a right-brain person to paint it. But if the painting was valuable and the artist lived a long way away, I'd want a left-brain person to work out the safest and most cost-efficient way of getting the painting from the artist's studio to my house.

That analogy might suggest that I regard right-brain thought as intrinsically more important than left-brain thought. I'm tempted for a nanosecond to agree with that: certainly the most exciting parts of life are usually driven by right-brain activity. But of course it's a ridiculous proposition; a moment's consideration will show that both types of thought are vital.

A good demonstration of the interdependence of right- and left-brain thought comes from ornithology. (That the study of birds is helpful in this may sound bizarre, but stick with me for a moment.)

Humans use both their eyes in much the same way. The advantage of having two eyes is that you get a sense of perspective, so you can judge distance better. And you have a spare if one gets damaged. But there are birds that use their left and right eyes quite differently. Here's why.

Most of the time a bird has just two preoccupations: finding food for itself is one; the other is not being food for someone else – in other words, avoiding predators. A bird wants to eat, and it wants to avoid being eaten.

In many bird species, the left eye is attuned specifically to find food. This makes it good at spotting small morsels at long range. In photographic terms, it works like a telephoto lens, with a narrow range of vision but a high degree of magnification. But the right eye works utterly differently. Its job is to spot predators before it gets spotted. So the right eye is good at looking anywhere and

everywhere for a bigger bird that may be thinking 'Lunch!' In photographic terms, it works like a wide-angle lens, with a very wide
field of view, but not much magnification.

If survival hinges on getting lunch before you become lunch for
someone else, this division of labour between the left eye and the
right eye is a brilliant concept. But you don't have to be an expert
ornithologist to grasp that each eye has to do its job. One on its own
is useless. And this has more to do with life in the office than you
might imagine.

**Left-brain activity, with its narrow look and
ability to magnify detail, is essential in work,
as well as in the rainforest. But so is right-
brain activity, with its breadth of vision and
ability to spot the unexpected.**

Yet we live in a world of work where left-brain virtues are greatly
overvalued and right-brain virtues are equally undervalued. In
almost every large business, the Finance Director (a left-brain job)
is effectively the Number Two to the Chief Executive. But hardly
any corporations even have a Design Director or a Creative
Director, and the most senior right-brain person might be a head
of marketing. While that's an important role, in most companies it's
certainly not that near the top of the power hierarchy.

This isn't an attack on Finance Directors, accountants and other emi-
nent left-brain people. Their ability to focus on narrow detail (like
the bird's left eye) is crucial. But (like the bird's left eye again) they're
not much good on their own: precision must be paired with vision.

It's revealing that when a public company shows its annual results
to the City, to financial analysts and shareholders, the Finance
Director is always there in support of the Chief Executive. His job

is to explain what *has happened*. But there's never anyone to support the Chief Executive in describing what *will happen*. It's OK to rationalise the past, but taboo to create the future.

And yet the track record of left-brain thinkers isn't that impressive. The collapse of Enron was one of the most spectacular falls from grace in the history of capitalism. But with the collapse of Enron went the collapse of their accountants, Arthur Andersen. Andersen's had been one of the world's top accountancy practices. Within a few months they had sunk without trace. How could the best and brightest of the world's left-brain thinkers have allowed themselves not to notice the massive fraud which undermined Enron, and indeed undermined themselves?

More recently, when Lehmans bank famously collapsed, and many other big banks had to be merged or saved by the state, what we saw was the result of too much left-brain thinking and not enough right-brain thinking. The banks which collapsed had all done their sums sensibly enough: they just never thought themselves to be vulnerable to a crisis of confidence. It was not a failure of accountancy; it was a failure of imagination. Their forecasts for the future were based, in a typically left-brain way, on an assumption that tomorrow was going to be a continuation of yesterday. They lacked the right-brain ability to think laterally, to understand that things can change suddenly. If there'd been a few less people with spreadsheets, and a few more saying 'What if . . . ?', the banking collapse might not have happened.

Alongside these left-brain catastrophes, we've had some right-brain triumphs. The extraordinary success of Apple, and the amazing way the iPhone, the iPad and the MacBook have invaded and changed our lives, must be one of the most significant cultural and social transformations in modern times. Most of that transformation is due to the remarkable vision of Steve Jobs, a right-brain thinker if ever there was one.

It makes me grumpy that in business life, left-brain attitudes predominate even though it's right-brain activity that generates most of the wealth.

This book is devoted to the belief that cold-blooded analysis is due for a kick in the backside, and it's high time to put passion, vision and creativity back where they belong: centre stage.

The office jungle – and how to hack your way through it

Office life often seems to offer an impenetrable jungle of problems. How many times do you go into work thinking about all those things you've got to do, and how little time there is to do them?

But the truth is that finding success at work is very simple: it depends much less on brilliant insights and much more on common sense than you might think. (Though I sometimes wonder why it's called 'common sense' since a good dose of basic sense is much rarer than it should be. 'Uncommon sense' would be a better term.)

The starting point to solving any problem is to stop worrying about it, and then to strip away all the surrounding fluff and concentrate on the basic essentials. The simpler your view of a challenge, the easier it is to get to grips with it.

Let's apply this thinking to life in the office jungle. It's a world which appears to be complex – but in truth there are really only three things you have to think about. What are those three things? They are:

How you deal with money
How you deal with people
How you deal with yourself

The first of these is unsurprising; how you make the money go round is obviously at the heart of any business. Accountants like to make the management of finance appear to be an arcane science which only they can understand. That's because it suits them to behave like business witch doctors with magical powers us ordinary mortals don't have. That's nonsense, as we will discover. I was a complete chump at maths at school, but I went on to run a company which made £180 million profit once I realised that all you need is a bit of confidence and a bit of clarity.

The true simplicity of understanding finance is brilliantly summarised by Mr Micawber – one of the great characters from Charles Dickens' *David Copperfield* – who famously declared:

'Annual income twenty pounds, annual expenditure nineteen nineteen and six, result happiness. Annual income twenty pounds, annual expenditure twenty pounds ought and six, result misery.'

No wonder Dickens had such a clear and simple grasp of how money works – his own father was imprisoned when he couldn't pay his debts.

So we'll push behind the accountant's curtain to see with Micawber-esque straightforwardness how to deal with money.

The second big thing to consider in the office is how to deal with people. Management and leadership are, at heart, just the skill of dealing with people. In truth, manipulating people is a far greater business talent than manipulating money. (Which is, incidentally, why Finance Directors usually make a great hash of things when they get promoted to Chief Executive.)

There's an endless array of different people you have to deal with: the staff that work for you, the boss that you work for, the bright talent you want to hire, the shareholders who own the company, the journalists who write rude things about it. Above all, the most important people you have to deal with are the customers on whom the business ultimately depends. We'll explore how to take on each of these groups and come out smiling.

Finally, you need to deal with yourself. This matters more than you might think. Many of the barriers to success lie in our own heads. Lucy Kellaway, an insightful journalist who writes with great wit and wisdom for the *Financial Times*, once did a brilliant piece about why some people make it to Chief Executive and others don't.

She considered the talents of the many businessmen and -women she'd met over the years (which, thanks to her job at the *FT*, was a lot) and studied what the real big hitters had which set them apart from the others. Her conclusion was startling: what the big hitters *did not* have in common was any greater intelligence than their understudies. But what they *did* have was a much greater degree of brute ambition and a much greater willingness to take risks to achieve that ambition.

They were no more clever than the people they'd beaten into

second place. But their hunger for the big prize was greater, and they were more willing to take risks to seize it.

So your own mindset is a much more powerful weapon than your brainpower. This is why 'How to deal with yourself' is the final, and most important, section of this book.

HOW TO DEAL WITH MONEY

Accountants, and how to beat them at their own game

If you have trouble sleeping, just repeat the words 'balance sheet' or 'profit and loss account' a few times and you'll soon be snoring soundly.

These accountant geek terms are mind-numbingly boring to us normal folk. But the problem is that if you're ambitious to get on at work, you need to understand this stuff, however ghastly that may seem. And – once you've got the hang of it – it's even modestly intriguing. After all, when you're watching sport, your eye instinctively turns to the scoreboard from time to time, and a balance sheet or a profit and loss account is simply a way of keeping the financial score.

But why do you need two different ways of keeping score? Is a balance sheet the same as a profit and loss account, and if not, what's the difference? Why do we need both?

Think about it in terms of your own personal finances. Let's say, before committing yourself to an expensive holiday, you want to know how well off you are. You'd look at what you earn each month and what you spend each month. If you're earning a bit more than you're spending, then you'll book your holiday. That's really your personal 'profit and loss account'. It's simply a measure of money coming in versus money going out.

Now imagine you're contemplating something much more ambitious – maybe buying your own flat. Just checking that you're earning a bit more than you're spending isn't enough if you need to find £250,000. You'll look at everything you own: maybe you've already got a smaller flat worth £150,000 and you've got £10,000 in your savings account. But as well as being clear about what you own, you also need to be clear about what you owe: you might have a mortgage on the flat with £100,000 still to pay, and maybe you have a £5,000 personal loan from your bank to help you buy your car.

So, add up the good news (that was £150,000 for the flat plus £10,000 savings) and you've got £160,000. Add up the bad news (£100,000 owed on the flat and £5,000 for the loan) and you've got £105,000. Take the bad news from the good – that's £160,000 minus £105,000 –and you're left with £55,000. That's what you have to start with before you try to raise the money for your new home. It's your net financial worth. And a balance sheet works exactly the same way. Of course, accountants will enjoy complicating it and peppering it with jargon, but that is really all a balance sheet is: a measuring of a company's overall worth, by comparing what it owes with what it owns.

Here's a real example of how this works in practice. A few years ago I was made CEO of a group of businesses which had just sold its most profitable division. I looked at the profit and loss account, and it showed that the businesses which remained in the group were losing money. Ouch! I then looked at the balance sheet. Because the group had banked a big sum as a result of the recent sale of their best division, the balance sheet was healthy: we had big cash reserves in the bank. Of course, those reserves would eventually drain away, because every year we made a loss, we'd have to take something out of the reserves to cover the loss. I worked out that if we carried on making a loss at the same rate, it would take about six years for the reserves to disappear.

My task as CEO was clear. I had to get the group back into profit in well under six years. But if I'd looked at the balance sheet on its own, I'd have had a misleadingly optimistic view of things; and if I'd looked at the profit and loss account on its own I'd have had a misleadingly gloomy view.

So you can see the balance sheet is really a measure of underlying strength (or not, as the case may be!) and the profit and loss account is a measure of what's going on in the here and now. As my example shows, one can be healthy, and the other unhealthy, at the same moment – which is why you need to keep an eye on both.

Now you get the principles of a balance sheet and a profit and loss account, but in practice you still have to know how to decode those strange and seemingly complicated documents. All you have to do is to ask someone in your finance department to talk you slowly through the documents. Don't say, 'I don't understand a balance sheet.' That won't do much for your credibility. Instead, say, 'Please take me through this balance sheet, and show me how you've put it together.' That flatters them: finance people love treating the rest of us as if we haven't really learnt to count yet, so you will appeal to the patronising side of their nature.

They will then try to blind you with science. Don't let them. Pester them with the simplest of questions, and you'll quickly find that the dark art of accountancy is really just financial common sense carefully packaged in complication.

Remember where we began in this chapter, and think about it in terms of your own personal money. The profit and loss account shows if you're spending more than you're earning; and the balance sheet shows what you're worth – what your reserves are.

Cash is King (and Ace, Queen and Jack)

Now you've mastered the distinction between a balance sheet and a profit and loss account, there's nothing else to learn, right? Not quite: there's one more crucial distinction to understand, and that is the difference between profit and cash.

Profit is a theoretical calculation – but only theoretical. Let's imagine your business has made a one million pound profit. That does not mean you've got one million in cash in the bank. You might have much more; you might have much less. Why?

You may have sold something to a customer, he's paid a deposit, you've delivered the product, and invoiced the outstanding amount. But the customer hasn't paid in full yet, though you're confident he'll pay soon. So the sale will show in the P&L (that's shorthand for Profit and Loss account) but you don't yet have all the cash in your bank.

You may have bought £100,000's worth of IT kit, which the accountants think will last five years. So in the accounts they'll put one fifth of the value, i.e. £20,000, in the accounts for the first year. The rest is spread (or 'depreciated' in their jargon) over the remaining four years. So the P&L will show £20,000 going out this year – but the bank account is already down by £100,000.

If you run a clothes shop, you might have bought £50,000's worth of T-shirts for the summer season, but you haven't sold any yet. Your bank account is already down by £50,000 because you've had to pay for them up front. But they won't show a penny of loss in the P&L, because the assumption is that you will sell them, and get your £50,000 back, plus a nice profit margin.

These are just three simple examples of how the theoretical profit and the actual cash can differ. Now imagine that in an average business, there might be thousands of these transactions going on at the same time, and you can quickly see that profit and cash can be miles apart.

Accountants and Finance Directors often spend hours agonising over the P&L, but it's vital to keep your eye on the cash too. Cash matters – for the very simple reason that the difference between a business which is bankrupt, and one which isn't, is that the bankrupt business has run out of cash.

It's perfectly possible to have a satisfactory P&L, but still go bust. It can happen if you've bought a lot of stock, but you can't sell it. It can happen if you pay your suppliers promptly, but your customers pay you slowly.

Bankruptcy is the moment when there simply isn't enough money in the bank account to pay the bills. Whether those bills are for rent, for stock, for salaries or for your staff, if you can't come up with the cash, you're out of the game.

It's not a good moment when the business you've been working on for years suddenly stops, when the staff who have been there for you go home with no job and no money. It's painful. It's only happened to me once, and I don't want it to happen twice. What makes it happen has little to do with the P&L and everything to do with the cash in the bank – or to be more precise, the cash *not* in the bank. 'Cash is king' is a truism in business, but it only got to be a truism because it is so very, very true.

If you're running a business, there's a million things to worry about – staff morale, last week's sales figures, recruiting a new receptionist while Polly has her baby . . . but the one thing I'd advise you to put at the top of your worry list is the cash.

To boost staff morale, you might want a party. To improve the sales figures, you might need some advertising. The new receptionist has to have a salary. This all needs cash. Cash is the blood of any business – and we know what happens when the blood drains away.

I once chaired a business which was losing money, but the board wanted to give salary increases to the staff to motivate them and stop them going to work for rivals. The staff were bright and deserved more. The risk of defection was real. But if we weren't making money now, I couldn't see how it was wise to spend more, and increase our losses. I had a seemingly endless series of argumentative meetings about this with the rest of the board. Eventually, I caved in. I told the board they could give a rise to the staff. And they could be as generous as they wanted.

But there was a condition: I asked the board to tell me what to say if, in a few months' time, someone on the staff stopped me in the corridor and said, 'I'm puzzled Mr Mavity: my bank has just said they've bounced my pay cheque and I don't have any money this month. I assume it's just a mistake?'

Suddenly the board realised that there is a direct and very real relationship between the decisions you make in a business and the amount of cash the business has. And there's an even more direct and real relationship between the cash in the company's account and the ability to keep going.

That's why 'cash is king' is a concept you should grasp, and then keep in your mind, day in day out.

As a postscript, you may wonder what happened to the company I chaired that couldn't afford to give rises? We didn't give the staff any rises, *but we got them all together and we told them why.* The effect was electric: far from being demotivated by not getting more money, they were highly motivated by being told the truth and treated like grown-ups. They worked hard, they worked as a team, and they got the business back into profit.

And then we gave them a well-earned pay rise.

PVC: fetishism or finance?

To most people, PVC is simply the name of a rather ugly but shiny material – with somewhat fetishistic overtones, if that's your thing.

But PVC isn't only the acronym for polyvinyl chloride (and if you had a name as cumbrous as that, you'd shorten it). It's also the acronym for a three-word phrase which goes to the heart of a how a business works: price, volume, cost.

Why are these three words so important? Because they are the three levers which decide how a business – yes, any business – makes money. There is nothing else which can drive the profit of a business. Or the loss, for that matter.

Imagine you're the head of a specialist, luxury sports-car maker. The *price* of each car you sell is £100,000. The *volume* of cars you sell is 1,000 units a year. And the annual *cost* of running your business comes to a total of £95 million. How much profit do you make?

Easy: take the price and multiply it by the volume, and that gives you your turnover for the year. In this case, that means a price of £100,000 multiplied by a volume of 1,000 units which makes a figure of £100 million. I'm not very good at sums with lots of noughts, but I think that's right. So your turnover (or sales, or income, or whatever you want to call it, but it's the total amount coming in) is £100 million. And your costs (which of course is the total amount going out) are £95 million.

Take the costs of £95 million away from the turnover of £100 million, and you've got £5 million left over. Which is your profit.

But in real life, business is more complicated than that, I can hear you say. Well, it truly isn't. It is just that simple. Some people may like to complicate it, but any and every business in the world is really driven by these three basic forces – price, volume, cost. There is nothing else.

Why is that so significant? Because whether you're running a large business or a small department, the mantra of PVC will help you unlock how you can make it more profitable. Think about the business in terms of the price you charge per product, the volume of products you sell, and the cost of making the business happen, and you have distilled the essence of the business into a clear, simple shape. It doesn't matter whether the business is General Motors or the sweetshop on the corner, the principles are still the same.

But what happens when you put those principles into practice? Assume for a moment that you sell dolls on a market stall. You know how many dolls you sell on a typical day (your volume) and you know how much you charge for each doll (your price) so you can work out your turnover. You also know how much you have to pay for the dolls, and how much you pay to rent the stall. So you know your costs. Now let's assume that you're not making enough profit to pay yourself a living wage. What do you do?

This is when PVC suddenly becomes valuable. The only way you can change things for the better is by raising the price of the dolls; by selling a greater volume of dolls; or by cutting your cost – which means buying the dolls more cheaply or spending less on rent. There is no other answer.

This may seem almost childishly simplistic. But believe me, the logic is flawless. And its simplicity is a good thing, not a bad thing. I've used the PVC method to analyse businesses a great deal larger and more complex than a market stall and it's an extraordinarily quick and clean way to understand what you need to do in order to make more profit.

The person who taught me this way of thinking about a business used to run one of the largest companies in Britain, and he's since been knighted for his services to industry; so if it's good enough for him, it's probably good enough for you and me.

Most people think that when a company's profit is low, you just need to sell more. In other words, you need volume. But the PVC discipline makes you think about all three drivers of profit, not just one. Cost and price are just as important as volume.

In fact, I'd argue that they're often more important. And it's worth understanding why.

You have the power to change price and cost. If you want to charge more for your product, you can. Sales may – or may not – fall as a result, but it is your choice. Equally, you can reduce cost. You can bargain with your suppliers for a better rate; you can move to cheaper premises; you can make do with fewer staff. Again, it's your choice. But making the volume go up is the customer's choice: they decide whether they are going to buy more, not you. Of course there are things you can do to influence them, such as advertising to them, but ultimately it is their choice not yours.

The implications of this are profound. In my experience, when business managers are faced with a lack of profit, their instinct is always to try to solve this by increasing their volume of sales. They don't want to cut costs because that involves painful decisions. They don't want to put the price up because they think that will frighten customers away. So they try to increase volume.

But, as we've just seen, that's much the hardest of the three levers to move, since it depends on other people's decisions. You may want customers to buy more but you can't make them. It's almost always much better to push the price up or push the cost down.

What about the fear that pushing the price up will frighten customers away? Of course that can happen, sometimes. But it depends how you do it. If the price is £19.90 just putting it up by 10 pence will make it £20 which somehow seems a lot more. But if the price is £19, you could put it up by 90 pence to £19.90 and it won't seem that much more.

At any rate, some products thrive on a high price: I don't think that Rolex watches would sell more if they dropped the price. On the contrary, it might well make them sell less, because the watch wouldn't seem so special. I know you don't buy a Rolex every day, but the same principle applies in more modest ways: I'd be happy to pay more for salami in a local deli than in Tesco because I'd assume it was better quality.

Before someone from Tesco grumbles, I accept that I might be wrong about this, but my perception is that a small, specialist shop would have a better product – and it's the perception that matters.

Some products are more sensitive to price than others. For a few years I was chairman of a big public relations company. The business had a high turnover, but low profits. That suggested to me that they simply weren't charging enough for the work they did. When I proposed that they increased their rates, there was a horrified reaction. They were all convinced that they would never win pitches for new business if they charged more. I argued that when a service is important, people want the best, not the best value. After all, if you needed an operation, you'd want the best surgeon, not the cheapest.

To make my point, I offered a prize to the first person to *fail* to win a contract because we were too expensive. It was many months before the prize was claimed; and in the meantime the profits of the company had risen fourfold – just because we had acquired the nerve to pitch our prices at a confident level.

When it comes to cutting costs, most managers freeze. They just can't deal with it. They will always rationalise that cutting costs will make the business worse – a smaller staff won't cope with the workload, if you spend less on something then quality will fall, etc., etc.

In my experience, the opposite is often the case: if you're compelled to work with fewer resources, it forces you to be more imaginative about how you do things.

The original Mini revolutionised car design for ever by finding new ways for a car to function which were simpler and cheaper – and better.

A friend of mine was once put in charge of a brand of soft drinks which were sold in glass bottles about the same size as a wine bottle. The brand had a colossal turnover, but it was still losing money. My chum wisely decided to see how he could cut costs.

He noticed that the bottles were packed in cardboard boxes, twelve bottles to a box, with cardboard dividers between the bottles to stop them breaking if they bashed against each other during transit. But he also noticed that the dividers were the same height as the bottles, even though the bottles tapered towards the top. So it was impossible for the top part of the bottles to bump up against each other. He simply stopped buying cardboard dividers the full height of the bottle, and instead bought ones which were two thirds the height. The bottles were just as safe in transit, but he'd saved a little bit of cardboard in each box. Multiply that small saving by the millions of boxes they sold each year, and he'd saved a lot of money.

A similar thing happened with boxes of matches: somebody noticed one day that you don't need a striker pad on both sides of the box – just one will do. Which is why boxes of matches today have one striker pad not two, and the shareholders are richer as a consequence. People always think that cutting costs makes things worse. But as these examples demonstrate, it's sometimes perfectly possible to make a big cost saving that makes no difference to the customers, and a very happy difference to the shareholders.

The emotional resistance people feel towards reducing costs is often intense. There are two reasons for this. Firstly, they are not imaginative enough to see that doing things more cheaply can also mean doing things better. Second, they think that cutting costs means cutting staff. Well, it often does, and cutting staff seems cruel. But if you have more people than you need, you are spending too much to get the job done, which means your price to the customer won't be competitive. Which means that in the long run you are putting everyone's job at risk. Cutting the staff back to the number you really need is horrible for those that go, but it protects the jobs of those that stay.

So PVC isn't just that shiny fabric with the fetishistic overtones. It's also short for 'price, volume, cost' – a brilliantly simple method of looking at how a business makes money, and understanding how that can be improved.

The annual budget: ritual or real life?

There is something strangely ritualistic about annual budgets. Even the Chancellor of the Exchequer is expected to pose awkwardly outside Number 11 every year, with that battered red box. It seems that the past and the red box are more important than the future and what's in the red box.

Budgets in business can be just as ritualistic: a predictable pattern of gentle bullying by management to get the executives to create a budget that looks good, but which they probably won't be able to deliver, punctuated by endless meetings studying massively detailed pages of figures.

The truth is that all those figures are merely forecasts – or guesses as I prefer to call them. I think 'guess' is a better word because it doesn't hide from the fact that we can't see into the future, whereas 'forecast' suggests something more scientific, something more innately credible. But if these figures are saying what will happen tomorrow, or next year, they're a guess and no more, so we might as well face up to that.

Am I being cynical? All I can say is that in a lifetime in business I've seen budgets for the year being missed more often than they're achieved, and when they are achieved it's usually by a whisker, but when they're missed it's often by a mile. So the budgeting ritual produces targets which are consistently overoptimistic. It's not surprising – people prefer to look at figures that are hopeful rather than at figures that are truthful. But while it's not surprising, it's also not helpful: if you start the year with an unrealistically optimistic budget, you'll spend the next twelve months disappointing your bosses and feeling increasingly demotivated yourself.

There is a different way of looking at budgets. Ignore the numbers. Yes, that's right – ignore all those pages of detailed and dreary figures. (We've just agreed they're guesswork anyway, so why spend time on them?) Instead, set out on one page a list of the all the *assumptions* in the budget.

How much have you assumed sales will grow? How much have you assumed you'll need to spend to get those sales? How many people have you assumed you'll need to handle that amount of turnover?

It's the quality of these assumptions which will drive the budget. Of course, the assumptions are guesses too – but the big question is whether they seem to be credible guesses, or whether they're just what we'd like to happen, as opposed to what we expect to happen.

When I review a budget I refuse to look at the actual numbers until I've agreed the assumptions. The reason is simple: if I start by looking at the profit target, and it's a bit low, I'll then look at the assumptions with a subconscious desire to improve the assumptions in order to raise the profit target. And we'll end up – yet again – with an unrealistic and overoptimistic budget.

So I just concentrate on the assumptions, and refuse steadfastly to look at the numbers. In fact I often ask people to do the assumptions first, and not to start the budget itself until we've agreed the assumptions.

When we've argued through the assumptions and agreed that they are as good as we're going to get, I then ask for the financial numbers to be prepared – and whatever they show is OK, because it's the result of the best assumptions we could get.

This process usually produces budget targets which are a bit lower (i.e. more realistic) than you'd get via the traditional method. But because they are more realistic, you've got a sporting chance of delivering to the shareholders, twelve months later, the profit you said you would deliver at the start of the year. So the shareholders get no nasty surprises, and you get the satisfaction of working through a year on a target which you truly can achieve.

How to write a business plan, and why you shouldn't rely on help from Socrates

S ooner or later you're going to have to write a business plan. Or is that a business strategy? And anyway, what's the difference?

Don't ask me to distinguish between a business plan and a strategy – different people use different titles for much the same thing. What I can tell you is that most business plans (or strategies . . .) I've seen are barely worth the paper they're written on. They're almost always long on information and short on ideas. A plan is a document which paves the way for action. Or it should be. But all too often, a so-called business plan is little more than a discussion document, which sets out a ton of facts and figures, but doesn't point clearly to the way ahead.

There is an old saying about the ancient Greek philosophers which goes: 'When Socrates spoke, they said, "How well he spoke" but when Demosthenes spoke, they said, "Let us march".'

In other words, Socrates concentrated on thought, almost as an end in itself, but Demosthenes was interested in making things happen: thought was a means to a practical end. It's a reasonable guess that if they were alive today, Socrates would be a management consultant, telling other people what to do, and Demosthenes would be a businessman, actually doing something himself.

If you're writing a business plan, think like Demosthenes not Socrates. The purpose of a business plan isn't just to define *what* you want to achieve, it's to define *how* you're going to achieve it.

So what goes in a business plan?

Start with a simple statement of your objective: what is your aim? That shouldn't take more than a sentence or two. If it's longer, it's too long, and you haven't got your objective clear in your own mind yet.

Then justify it. Why do you want to achieve that goal? Again, if the answer isn't brief, it's not right either. Detail is important in a plan, but only to support the main idea. You need to spell out that big idea clearly first.

Next, show a simple financial plan. How much money will the project earn; how much will you need to invest to generate those earnings; how much profit will it make; and finally when will that profit arrive?

It's worth being self-critical about this bit. There's a great temptation to be overly optimistic about how much money will come in from sales; and equally optimistic about how little you'll have to spend to get those sales. Look honestly at what you've put down, and ask yourself if you're being realistic. Then ask yourself if the amount of money you're asking for seems sensible against the amount of profit you expect to make. Is the level of risk reasonable, against the reward you hope for? If things go a bit wrong, does it still make decent money? Finally, how long does it take to make profit?

This last one matters more than you might think. Plans which produce profit very quickly in theory hardly ever work that smoothly in practice. Plans which take a long time to produce profit may simply not be worth doing.

Once you're happy that you have a clear objective, a credible justification, and a sensible financial proposition, then you need to get into how the plan will be achieved. *What are you actually going to do in order to make it happen?*

Let's imagine an example. You're going to launch a new range of kitchen utensils. You need to describe how you're going to get the products made, which shops will sell them, how you're going to get those shops to stock them, how you're going to get the products to the shops, and how you're going to publicise the new products.

Make a list of all the hurdles that stand between you and a sale to the customer – making, distributing, advertising, etc. – and summarise in one paragraph, for each of these hurdles, how you're going to surmount that hurdle.

Many business plans I see are filled with guff about what the competition is doing, how big the market is, and all sorts of other worthy stuff. But none of it is really that relevant. What matters is not what your competitors are doing, what matters is what you intend to do, and how you intend to do it.

If you were an army general planning an invasion of enemy territory, you wouldn't want to wade through reams of information, let alone pages of spreadsheets. You'd just set out as clearly as you could what you wanted to achieve and what you were going to do, in a very practical way, to achieve it.

It helps to think of a business plan in the same way. It's not an academic thesis, it's a working document, defining where you want to be and how you're going to get there.

The simpler it is, the better it is. And when in doubt, remember to emulate Demosthenes, and leave Socrates well alone.

It's no use doing the work if you don't get paid

People are weirdly shy about asking for money – even when it's money for work they've done and are entitled to be paid for. When I worked in advertising there was a sense that to chase a client to pay a bill was a sign of weakness, as if the firm wasn't strong enough to carry on unless the bill was paid.

The truth is that no firm, whether it's the Coca-Cola Company or the local window cleaners, is strong enough to carry on indefinitely if it doesn't get paid for what it does. The Coca-Cola Company could carry on unpaid for a lot longer than the window cleaners, but reality will catch up with everyone in the end.

And if someone offered your company an important contract, but said, 'We'll agree a fee for this but of course I'm not going to pay it,' you'd assume they were mad.

If you don't get paid, the business collapses. It really is that simple. No one can defy gravity. But to get paid, you usually have to ask.

While there is often a feeling that pressing for payment shows anxiety, I think the reverse is true. It's a sign of self-belief. You have a business to run, you're confident about what you do, you expect to get paid for that work, and promptly too. If you're quite tough about running a business in a businesslike way, you'll be respected for that.

Every good business gets its invoices out quickly and expects them to be paid on time. But getting a bill paid can take a bit of determination. My experience is that if there is a small delay in getting paid, everyone wants to be gentle and give the people who owe you money the benefit of the doubt. The result is never what you hope for: they don't appreciate your kindness, they exploit it. So the debt drags on, as you've already shown that you tolerate delay. It's much better to be firm about payment the second the money is overdue.

When I was running my own advertising agency I had a healthy paranoia about getting paid on time – as you would understand, since it was my own money on the line. Once we had a big outstanding debt from one of the largest food companies in the world who were also one of our largest clients. We kept phoning their accounts department, sending them copies of the invoices they'd claimed to have mislaid, and we still didn't get paid. Everyone at my end was nervous about harassing such a powerful organisation. Everyone except me, that is. If I buy one of their products from the supermarket, I give them the money when I take the product. In the same way, I expected them to pay for their advertising when they get it, not months later.

But it was clear that we had fought the battle with their accounts department, and lost. If they hadn't paid after ten phone calls, they wouldn't pay after eleven. Accounts departments are brilliant at explaining why you haven't been paid – less brilliant at solving that problem. It's usually quicker to go over their head. So I rang the PA of the Chief Executive.

I said to her, 'I just wanted to let you know that the motorbike is on its way, and it should be there by noon.'

She was mystified: 'What motorbike?' she asked.

'The one to collect the cheque for the money you owe us,' I replied.

To want to be paid didn't make us look weak; it made them look foolish. The PA to the Chief Executive in any company is a powerful person, good at getting their own way, otherwise they wouldn't have the job. In this case, the threat of the PA's boss being confronted in reception by a motorbike messenger demanding money (possibly in front of all the other folk in reception that day) had exactly the effect I wanted. By the time the motorbike messenger arrived, the cheque was there too.

I've never seen anyone lose respect by asking for their due. I've often seen people lose money by failing to.

Irving Berlin, one of the great songwriters of the jazz age, was once asked, 'Which comes first, Mr Berlin, the words or the melody?'

Berlin's answer was simple: 'The contract comes first.'

He clearly thought it was possible to be businesslike and creative at the same time. It's an idea we should imitate.

Does the morality go down as the profits go up?

A recurring theme in this book is profit: how to make it, and how to improve it. Yet we live in times where capitalist values are being called into question. The bankers we once thought of as sober guardians of our savings are now often revealed as little more than greedy gamblers. Pension funds don't always seem to have enough money to honour their commitments. Whole countries are scrounging off richer neighbours to pay off debts that they should never have incurred in the first place. The dream of a gradual, but inexorable, rise in the prosperity of Western nations has suddenly turned into a nightmare of anxious austerity.

The collapse of Enron showed us that a company admired as one of the great pillars of the world's largest economy was little more than a gigantic fraud. More recently, the revered Goldman Sachs has been found out publicly pushing an investment to its clients that it was privately betting on to fail. Who can we trust?

In this nervous world, the very idea of big profits makes us feel a bit uncomfortable. When a large corporation announces a huge rise in profits, there's a tendency to wonder what lies underneath. Do we still believe that the profit motive is a healthy force in our society?

Before we get too holier-than-thou about all of this, it's worth understanding what happens to profit once it has been created. Let's imagine that one year a large business makes a profit of £600 million. What then happens to that money? The money generally goes in three different directions: some goes in tax, some goes in dividends, some stays in the business.

Let's explore that. Our company making a £600 million profit will typically have to pay tax at around 30 per cent. So £180 million of that profit goes to the government. Now some people don't like tax; they'd love to pay less, and some even employ clever accountants to find ways to pay less. But the truth is that tax is what pays for our schools, our hospitals, our roads. Tax is what pays the wages of policemen, teachers, nurses, doctors. Tax, unlovely though it may seem, is the fuel on which a civilised society runs.

Which means that when a company announces higher profits, one implication is that more money is going in tax to make our schools, our hospitals, our whole nation a little bit better resourced. So you, and all of us, benefit from that tax payment.

What about the money that goes in dividends? Let's imagine that our £600 million profit company decides to pay £150 million of that profit in dividends: doesn't that mean that a lot of rich shareholders are just getting richer?

Beware of getting too sanctimonious. Consider first who those shareholders actually are. Usually they will be big institutions like pension funds and insurance companies, who have bought their shares as an investment. Who benefits from that? You do. If your pension is going to pay out when you retire, the pension fund which has your savings has got to make good investments before you retire.

Don't forget that it was investment by shareholders which funded the business in the first place. The company, and the employment it gives, couldn't happen without money to launch it. That money came from shareholders, who took a risk in funding the business when it began – which is why you shouldn't begrudge them a return on that risk investment, when the company has earned it.

So, this imaginary company has paid out £180 million in tax – which we're pleased about, when we reflect that this tax is helping to fund our schools and our hospitals.

Then the company's paid out £150 million in dividends to shareholders. Which we're also pleased about, when we reflect that it may be underpinning our pension, and it was the shareholder's investment which made the business possible in the first place.

But what about the rest? There's still £270 million left. Where does that go?

It goes back into the business, that's where. It strengthens the reserves, it increases the pool for investment, it enables more talent to be hired, and it creates more funds to reward the talent that's already there.

So that's what happens when a company makes good profits. The business is healthier; the shareholders (maybe including your pension fund) get a good return on their investment; and there's a positive nudge to the tax revenues which pay for our society.

And that is why I celebrate big profits, rather than condemn them.

Of course, it's very different in a case like Enron, where there was the pretence of big profits on the surface, but underneath lay an elaborate – and fraudulent – structure of dishonest accounting to make the profits look much better than they were.

Mind you, the Enron case does beg a question about our big accountancy practices: how could these large and respected firms fail to notice the kind of wrongdoing which went on at Enron? It makes me wonder whether accountants aren't too busy telling their clients what they want to hear and not busy enough telling the public what we need to know.

But most companies aren't Enron. Most companies are working hard, and honestly, to improve their profits. When they do, I'm pleased – not just for them, but for the society around them. I hope I've encouraged you to feel the same way.

HOW TO DEAL WITH **PEOPLE**

It's no use dealing with the money if you can't deal with the people

Much of office life seems to be about dealing with money – sales figures, profit, cash flow, budgets, and more. But at the heart of every business are people. You can't get sales without customers buying, and customers are people. You can't get the product to sell without people to make it. You can't even have a business in the first place without shareholders to invest in it, and they are people too.

How you manage the people around you is at the very heart of how you do your job. Different people need to be managed in different ways. Yet my experience tells me that those who are good at dealing with the boss – managing up – are often not at all good at dealing with people under them in the hierarchy – managing down. The reverse is true too: people who manage down well often handle their boss much less well. But you succeed at one and fail at the other at your peril.

This is neatly illustrated by a true story from New York in the 1960s.

Modern advertising was largely invented by a brilliant American adman called Bill Bernbach. He set up his own business, Doyle Dane Bernbach, and their work quickly became recognised as original and creative. At first, they won small, quirky accounts; large corporations were suspicious of them. Then their distinctiveness could no longer be ignored and they started to win work for giant companies like Avis and Volkswagen. Suddenly, Doyle Dane Bernbach was a big business itself. And it needed more structure. Bernbach hired a new Chief Executive from one of the established New York agencies, and briefed him to organise things to cope with a much larger workload. The new CEO started by restructuring the board. He called a board meeting where grandiose titles were dished out like jellies at a kid's party. He went round the room announcing, 'Fred, I'd like you to be Global Head of Creative; Max, I'd like you to be Worldwide Vice-President of Media . . . ' and so on. All the people who reported to him were awarded roles and titles of magnificent status.

When he'd finished, he realised – too late – that the one person he'd left out was Bernbach himself. Sheepishly he turned to him and said, 'Well Bill, I guess that leaves you. What title would you like?'

Bernbach looked at him stony-faced, paused two beats, and said, 'Owner'.

It was not a good start for the new CEO. He'd flattered the people who reported to him, but he'd ignored the man to whom he reported. Unsurprisingly, he didn't last at the agency as long as Bill Bernbach did.

It's a perfect example of the plain truth that you have to be able to deal with the people below you *and* the people above you. The irony is that the skills you need to manage up are pretty much the same as the skill you need to manage down: the difference lies in the motivation.

People who are not that confident manage up badly because they are fearful, and nervous people don't inspire confidence. But by the same token, they are often sensitive to the people under them.

People who are confident and ambitious often manage up well, because they work at it and because confidence breeds confidence. But they are frequently bad at managing down, I suspect because they just don't care as much. When you're climbing a ladder you look at the rungs above you, not the rungs below. But bosses aren't stupid and if they see someone who manages the generals well but shows little care for the troops, it will go against them.

So you need to define which type you are, and discipline yourself to attack the half of the job you don't do well. If you deal well with upstairs, you must force yourself to show concern for the lot down-stairs; not because you're nice, but because you're ambitious. You won't get to where you want if you can't show sensitivity to those you lead. If you deal well with downstairs, you have to drive your-self to show confidence and maturity with the people you report to. Again, it's not a choice – it's something you have to do if you're going to make it.

You may think I'm asking for the leopard – you, in this case – to change its spots. Well, perhaps I am, and I know how difficult that can be. But if you want to succeed you have to do both jobs: you have to be able to look up and to look down. It's less a question of acquiring new skills and more a question of forcing yourself to apply skills you already have to an audience you've undervalued. It's a bit like losing weight or giving up smoking. You don't need to learn a talent, you just have to have real determination to do what you know you need to do.

At this point, you may be thinking that someone at the start of his career doesn't have anyone to manage. That's true at the trainee stage, but if you're bright you'll soon have someone to guide, however junior they may be. And that will grow as you grow. You may also be thinking that the Chief Executive doesn't need to worry about this stuff: he doesn't have a boss. Wrong. In fact he has several bosses: the shareholders who own the business. Chief Executives who forget this inconvenient truth tend not to last as long as those who do. There's a great Bob Dylan song, 'Gotta Serve Somebody' which is about the notion that however powerful you are, you are still always accountable to somebody. And Dylan is right.

I said a moment ago that the skills of managing up and the skills of managing down are actually very similar – but what are those skills?

There are three big skills you need to deal with those above you, and those below you. They are: clarity of objective, clarity of communication, and straight dealing.

Let's explore these. Clarity of objective means what it says: being very clear about what it is that you want to get done. If you're managing down, you need to be clear about what you want others to do. If your people understand what the goal is, they are much more likely to achieve it. If you are managing up, you need to be clear about what you want to do. That's because when you are managing up, you are effectively explaining to your boss what you are setting out to do and how well you are doing it. That starts with being clear about your aims.

Clarity of communication is also pretty self-explanatory. But that does not mean it's always achieved. Look at what goes on in your own office and ask yourself how often problems are caused by people failing to be clear about what they want done, having muddled objectives, or just changing their minds. See what I mean? A good test is to write down the objective of a project in one sentence before you talk to others. If you can explain it simply to yourself, you can probably explain it simply to them too.

'Simply' is a key word in this: if your one sentence turns out to be three or four, don't brief anyone else – you haven't understood it yourself yet.

Lastly, straight dealing – what do I mean by that?

If you're managing up, you want your boss to be pleased with you. So the temptation is to tell him all the good news. The bad bits get underplayed, or even left out. If that ploy works, it only works for about ten minutes. The truth always comes out in time. When it does, if you've brushed bad news under the carpet, you're in trouble. Of course, facing bad news is tough too. But once you've confronted the problem, things start to get better. If you hide bad news, things can only get worse.

There's a saying that it takes courage to tell truth to power. That is undeniable. But it takes stupidity *not* to tell truth to power – because your weakness will be found out and will come back to haunt you.

Don't forget that people in power are used to stuff being shown to them with the problems hidden, because most people are cowardly and are frightened of being the messenger of trouble. So if you're brave enough to tell the boss the bad news, you'll be in a good minority. The boss may be angry about the bad news at the time, but you'll earn respect for being one of the few who told the painful truth.

Straight dealing matters when you are managing down, too. People at work are often surprisingly insecure about their role and how it relates to the people around them. If you're not completely straight with them, they'll find out the truth eventually, with two results. First, their insecurity will increase, which won't help them or you: anxious people don't do good work. Second, they won't trust you again. You've turned an employee into an enemy.

Of course, being straight about the good stuff is easy. Telling someone that they've got the raise they wanted, or telling the boss you've won the contract you were after are both ridiculously simple tasks.

The difficulty comes when you're being straight about the bad stuff. It's crucial here to find some positive to sit with the negative. If he didn't get the raise he wanted, maybe he'll get that reviewed again in six months; or maybe nobody got an increase because the economy is tough. There has to be some kind of consolation. And if you're telling the boss that you didn't win the contract, are there other contracts you're chasing, or is there an existing customer who's spending more?

Always find some reason for optimism to sit alongside the disappointment. How you do it is up you. When things are tough, honesty is essential, but it has to be married to hope.

Being interviewed: terror or triumph?

B eing interviewed can be terrifying, but it can also open the door for a new career. It's a skill worth working at. There are, I believe, three things you must concentrate on.

First, be interested in *them*. Learn as much as you can about their company in advance. If they own stores, make a point of visiting one in an out-of-the-way place, not just the one on Oxford Street. If they make products, buy some, use them, and have an opinion about them. Get their company report, study it, and ask questions about it. Above all, don't just research them on the internet – that's the lazy man's way, and you need to demonstrate a bit of effort and initiative.

Second, match their need to your skill. Every job requires some particular talents. For a finance role it may hinge on numeracy, for a sales role it may hinge on charm, but whatever the job is, there will be a few key talents you'll need to do it well. Your interviewer will be looking for evidence that you have those talents, and usually they define that by looking at your previous experience for that reassurance. In simple terms, they'll be thinking, If he's done it before, he can do it again.

What you have to do is to identify the needs they have, and show that you have the gift to match those needs. This is something you can plan in advance. It should be clear from their brief what they need; you just have to consider how you can present yourself as the answer to that question. Sometimes that's obvious – if your own experience has covered tasks which prove you can meet their need, you just have to say so. But often you're not a perfect fit. Maybe you're a bit too young, or maybe your experience has been in a different industry. Here's where you need to think laterally. If you're too young, accept that, but point to your energy and ambition, and your willingness to learn fast.

If your experience comes from somewhere different, think how the underlying talent required may still be the same, and focus on that.

Remember that interviewers are a cautious breed: subconsciously they're much more inclined to concentrate on avoiding mistakes than grasping opportunities. So your ability to reassure them that you have the skill to match their need – in plain English, that you know how to do the job – is crucial.

In an interview, the mood of the encounter is often as important as the actual content. If the chemistry is good, you're well on the way to getting the prize. So, how do you create good chemistry?

Be short in your answers. Keep your responses simple; it's amazing how often the inherent nervousness of an interview leads to long, complicated answers – which are very off-putting. Equally, crisp, simple answers are confidence-inspiring.

As well as being short on answers, be long on listening: it's flattering to be listened to.

Be enthusiastic. Don't overdo it, in a clumsy and obvious way, but you'd be surprised how often candidates fail to convey a straightforward enthusiasm to win the job. Remember, enthusiasm is infectious.

Here's a good example of that. Claudia Rosencrantz, a friend of mine and a very brilliant TV producer, started her career as a lowly researcher for a newspaper. Then she heard about an opening at London Weekend Television – at that time, one of the UK's top TV programme makers. She sent them a long letter, explaining how her talents were right for that job – quite brave for someone with zilch experience in television. She got her interview, and Claudia being Claudia, she prepared thoroughly for every question they could ever throw at her. Come the interview, the nervous but ambitious young Claudia sat facing an inquisitorial panel of three interviewers. And she dealt with their questions well, until the end, when she was asked the one question she hadn't anticipated.

'What questions would you like to ask us?' the panel enquired.

Claudia was floored. She was brilliantly rehearsed for any question she might get, but she hadn't expected to be asking questions herself. She paused, thought hard for a few seconds, and then said, 'I only have one question. Can I have the job?'

Three days later, the job offer came in the post. Claudia went on to be a major figure in British TV production, and many of the programmes you enjoy now were created by her. But it all began with a cheeky bit of raw enthusiasm.

Finally, be confident. You might not feel it inside, but you must radiate it outside. They want to feel confident about you. That's more likely to happen if you're confident about you too.

The art of the interview – from the other side of the table

When people talk about how to handle an interview, the presumption is always that *you* are the candidate. In truth, I think being the interviewer is just as testing as being the interviewee. And it's important: when you're interviewing, it's because there's a gap to fill. If you fail to fill the gap you're an incompetent manager, but fill the gap with the wrong person and you have trouble in store.

Most interviewers love talking about their business, and rationalise this on the grounds that the candidate needs to know. The only thing they enjoy more is talking about themselves. But that's all an egocentric waste of time. You're not there to talk, you're there to find out. That means you're asking questions, not speech-making.

If you talk more than you listen, you'll learn nothing about the candidate. Unfortunately, they'll learn something about you: that you're too self-important to take seriously. So don't lecture, just ask and listen.

But what questions should you ask? To resolve that, you need to be clear about what you want to learn. Inconveniently, what you want to learn is how well they'll do the job you need to fill, but that's the one thing you'll never know, because we can't predict the future. So you need to find as much circumstantial evidence as you can.

Ask them about what they've done in their previous career which might be relevant to your vacancy. Encourage them to give specific relevant examples, not to talk generally about their career. If they're good, they'll talk about what they have done in a way which focuses on your needs. And if they talk endlessly about their past without linking that to your problems, be very wary.

Next, ask them why they want the job. The good ones will tell you what they like about the job you're offering. The bad ones will go on and on about what they dislike about the job they're leaving.

Finally, ask them a bit about themselves. Never mind their professional skills – what kind of human being are they? Are they ambitious? Are they going to be fun to work with?

This is all very conventional stuff, you may say. And you'd be right. But an interview is like any other research; before you get the information, you think having the information is everything. Then, when you get the information, you realise that what matters is how you interpret it. And it's in the interpretation that the real skill lies.

I suggest you concentrate on two simple but important criteria.

First, how did they handle themselves in the interview? Good candidates are quick to the point, and give short, simple answers. They admit shortcomings, and when they don't know the answer they say they don't know. But they put this in a positive tone, and say clearly what they can offer. They talk more about future opportunity than past experience. And they make the encounter a warm human experience. If they're comfortable in their own skin, and comfortable with you, they'll probably be good at handling the myriad of other people they'll have to deal with when they get the job.

Above all, do they exude enthusiasm? Someone who really wants the job is far more likely to do it well. There's a saying, simplistic but scarily true, that people are either radiators or drains. Only hire radiators; leave drainage to the plumbers.

Second, forget about the technical skills needed for the job, and define the temperamental skills you need. Some jobs need determination, some a fascination with detail, some need imaginative flair. Be clear about the personality type you want. Then measure the candidate against that. If they're not a good fit emotionally, it's irrelevant whether they're a good fit technically. But if they are a good emotional fit, *if the personality feels right*, you've found your answer. Of course it helps if they have good and relevant technical experience, but even if they haven't, don't worry – they'll learn that fast enough when they're doing the job.

Finally – and this really matters – if it gets to the stage when you've chosen them and you're negotiating terms, remember they are still being interviewed. On two occasions, I've found a really impressive candidate for a senior job, but they were both pedantically over-thorough about agreeing the details of the deal. I should have seen the warning signs. But I didn't. I told myself that they were entitled to be a bit pedantic about their career. Yet the truth is that any job offer requires a leap of faith on both sides: you can't iron out every potential eventuality in advance. Someone who is slow to decide before taking the job will be just as slow to decide afterwards.

And so it proved with both these two individuals. When they finally signed up I heaved a sigh of relief. It should have been a sigh of anguish. Both proved to be woefully indecisive in action – a cardinal failing in any manager. One lasted seven months, the other five, before I had to say 'enough is enough'.

So please, learn from my mistake. If you find the right candidate, and they're nitpicking and slow over signing the deal, you haven't found the right candidate after all.

It's painful to own up to that at the time. But it's a lot more painful not to.

Deep end or shallow end: which is the best way into the pool?

I've noticed in office life that when someone new joins, a strange thing tends to happen. Does the new person get stuck into their new job immediately? Oh no, they usually get sent on an 'induction programme'. This is an introductory course, often of quite a few weeks, spent with different people and departments in the business, being told about the job, meeting the people they'll have to work with, and so on. The idea is that you understand the job before you do it.

On the face of it, this seems eminently sensible. But in my view it's anything but sensible. Let me explain why. There are three very specific reasons why I believe induction usually ends up doing more harm than good.

Firstly, it simply doesn't do the job it's supposed to do. The encounters that a new arrival has with their colleagues during an induction period are inevitably hollow. Because the new person is not yet really engaged with their task, they don't know what questions to ask. So the dialogue they have is little more than small talk.

You don't learn how to solve a problem by hearing someone else describe it to you, you solve it by getting down and dealing with it yourself.

The second problem is an extension of the first. If the induction period does not achieve much, it becomes a waste of everybody's time. And in business, a waste of time is also a waste of money.

The third problem, however, is the most fundamental, and it has to do with the psychology which underlies induction programmes.

What message does an induction programme send to the new arrival?

On the surface, it is saying: 'We want to you to do well, so we're giving you the best chance of that by training you up before we unleash you on your new responsibilities.'

But is it really saying that, beneath the surface? Isn't it actually saying: 'We know best. You can't do the job unless we explain it to you. You're here to learn from us. We don't expect to learn from you.'

The real underlying message is patronising and undermining. It implies that the company has a predetermined style, which new people have to learn before they can perform. So the new arrival's role is to conform to company style, not help develop it.

The psychology of this is born of fear: a new arrival is a threat. An induction programme is a mechanism to contain that threat by inculcating the new arrival with existing ideas and implicitly discouraging them from generating new ideas of their own. Induction seeks to control, not to liberate.

You may think I'm taking this all a bit too seriously. But the way a new person starts in a business can have a real effect on how they develop. A cautious and fearful start contributes to a cautious and fearful culture.

It speaks of too much time spent thinking about what might go wrong, and not enough time spent thinking about what might go right.

I'm greatly in favour of throwing people in the deep end of the pool, so they learn to swim immediately, not gradually introducing them via the shallow end, with all the nervousness that implies.

When a new person arrives, they only need to know two things: where the loos are and where the coffee machine is. They already know the brief for the job, since that will have been talked to death in the interview process.

Everything else they'll learn best by finding out for themselves, not by being told.

And being thrown in the deep end is confidence inspiring. The coded message you're getting is: 'We're not going to tell you how to do it: we trust you to find your own way.'

It not only implies trust, it also implies urgency – 'we've got to get on with this'.

The brighter people are, the more they respond to the deep-end approach. But the benefits of this style are not restricted just to the new arrivals; the style also influences the culture of the whole business. It shapes the culture towards trust and confidence, towards wanting to hear new answers. It shapes the culture away from caution and perpetuating existing systems.

Which type of business would you rather work in?

Don't buy a dog and bark yourself: the art of delegation

As you climb up the slippery slope of office life, you'll suddenly find yourself in the odd position of having someone reporting to you. Instead of doing the work yourself, you'll have the job of getting them to do it for you.

Sounds easy, doesn't it? Yet relinquishing the task to someone else when you've been used to doing it all yourself can be surprisingly difficult. Like much of office work, nobody trains you or explains to you how to delegate. It's just assumed that somehow you'll magically know, without any previous guidance.

If you're at all ambitious, you're probably also a bit perfectionistic. Which means when you get someone else to do the job, you're pretty certain that they won't do it the way you would, and they won't do it as well. That in turn means that it's easy to be trapped into explaining so thoroughly how you want the job done that it would probably have been quicker to do it yourself.

When you're delegating to someone, the person you need to worry about isn't them – it's yourself.

You have to think first about the art of delegation as a job in itself. Like every job, it benefits from some planning and preparation before you launch into it.

Start by writing down what the purpose of the job is, and what a successful outcome would be. This is for you, not them: the aim is to get your thoughts clear before they get involved. Then check your brief. Is it simple, and is it clear? If 'yes', that's fine. If 'no', work on it until it is both simple and clear. A little time spent at the start will save hours later.

Then you can give your brief. Do that verbally, using your notes, and give them the written notes to take away. Avoid the pitfall of telling them too much detail. It's far better, and more motivating for them, to let them discover the detail by asking you questions.

Above all, resist the temptation to tell them how to do the job. Define to them very clearly the result you want, but let them work out the best way of getting that result. Bad delegators radiate doubt and worry by briefing in great detail in a way that implies they're not sure you can do it without their help. Good delegators give you the freedom to solve the problem in your own way.

Both techniques become self-fulfilling. Bad delegators show anxiety, which is infectious, and the job gets done badly. (And the bad delegator thinks, I feared this would happen, without realising it's his fault.) Good delegators trust you to succeed, which is empowering, so you do succeed.

Many people have a bit of a death wish about delegation. They believe they can do the job well, and they start to think that means that no one else can do it well. If you're a bit insecure, it's uncomfortable to accept that others may be as good as you.

Somewhere in the dark depths of a bad delegator's psyche is a hope that the job will fail, thereby proving their unique talent. It takes a bit of confidence to enjoy other folk succeeding, and not see it as a threat.

Given that a lot of business people are insecure, it's no surprise how many poor delegators there are. But if you're willing to give a bit of trust to others, you'll get good work out of them, and you'll be the beneficiary.

Sir Gerry Robinson, who transformed Granada Group from a catastrophe into one of the most powerful companies in Britain, was a brave and brilliant delegator. He told you clearly what he hoped you would achieve, but he said nothing about how you should achieve it. When you left his office after the briefing, you realised that he hadn't given you a budget, or a timetable, or any guidelines, or any advice. The strong implication was that you wrote your own rules. He gave you all the power. But in so doing, he also gave you all the responsibility. It inspired you with confidence, but it generated a real pressure to perform as well. You thought you *could* do it. But you also thought you *must* do it.

Gerry once briefed me to take over a travel business which was struggling. He wanted me to get it into profit. How I did that was up to me. A few weeks later, we were talking, and he asked how this project was going. I explained that the incumbent head of the business was a very respected and experienced guy in the travel trade, yet the business was failing. Should I keep him because of his expertise, or should I replace him because he wasn't delivering?

Gerry looked at me with that charming Irish smile, and then he said, 'That's a tough one, Roger. I'm glad I don't have to make that decision.'

The message was clear: it's your task, you sort it out, don't ask me for help – rely on yourself. It was inspiring, and a bit scary at the same time.

I decided that a brave decision that failed would look better than an easy decision that failed.

So out went the expert, and in came someone new: someone I deliberately chose because he knew nothing about the business, but was bright and open-minded.

The business was making good money within a few months, for the first time in twenty years. Gerry's determination not to give advice, to force me to work out my own answer, was vindicated.

Is there life beyond email?

You may find this hard to believe, but there was a time when email did not exist. That was many years ago, when dinosaurs roamed the earth – about 1990 to be more precise. Amazingly, the wheel was invented, penicillin was discovered, and the Taj Mahal was built, all without the help of email. But in a modern office, everyone is endlessly reading emails, sending emails, worrying about emails. If they're at their desk, they'll be staring at emails on a screen, and if they're away from their desk, they'll be looking nervously for emails on their phone, lest withdrawal symptoms set in.

How did this new form of electronic letter-writing (which is really all it is) take over our lives so quickly and yet so completely?

The answer is that emails are quick and emails are easy. Astonishingly so. Because of that, they are a highly efficient way of getting information around fast.

But if you compare the flavour of a slow-cooked casserole with something heated up in two minutes in a microwave, you'll know that fast isn't everything. Pace matters, but so does quality.

The advantages of email are obvious; the disadvantages are more hidden and so more insidious. Emails are words without people; they are content without tone.

Tone matters. Here's a simple test to demonstrate the point. Say 'thank you' a few times, with a different tone each time. You can make 'thank you' sound genuinely grateful. But you can also make it sound perfunctory, sarcastic, even bitter. What gives tone to a statement is the timbre of your voice and your body language. If I say 'I love you' in a clipped voice with an expressionless look on my face, it's clear that I mean the opposite.

Emails are deaf to these nuances. And it's a one-way street, whereas real communication is a dialogue. You know what *you're* saying, but you don't know how it's being *received*. When you were a kid, did you ever practise tennis against the garage door? Emailing is a bit like that: you just get one side of the debate.

Don't get me wrong: I'm not decrying the huge usefulness of the email in office life. But I am saying that emails are limited. They are communication without mood, and they are communications without immediate reaction, because the audience is held at long range.

There is a type of communication which doesn't have these drawbacks. It's called talking to people. You probably do it a bit already, but I recommend that you try it more often at work. It amazes me in the office to see people sending emails to someone two desks away, when they could simply walk a few feet and have a real conversation.

I deplore most business jargon, but there is one jargon term I respect. That's MBWA, which is an acronym for 'management by walking about'. I make a point, every day I'm in the office, of wandering about the building once or twice and talking to whomever I meet.

As a means of communication it's not an alternative to email, but it is a brilliant addition. It's spontaneous, it's human, it's friendly, it's everything an electronic memo can never be. You learn a lot of stuff you'd never get to learn if you're hiding behind a laptop screen. And the people you work with get to see you as a human being, not just another office drone.

You may think it's easy for the boss to do that, but hard for a beginner. That's true, up to a point, but don't let that blind you to the power of human, rather than electronic, contact – even when you're at the start of your career and trying to get through to someone more senior. As a boss, I know that if someone relatively junior sends me an email, I'll deal with it as quickly and painlessly as I can, along with the mass of other emails I'll get that day. But if that junior person asks to *see me and talk to me face-to-face,* he'll make far more impact on me.

If you are a beginner seeking a dialogue with a boss, you'll need a good reason, as well as a bit of courage and a bit of tact. And if you do get the appointment, be sure to make your point as quickly and simply as you possibly can. But realise that a good boss will secretly admire a beginner who's a little pushy, provided they make their point with quickness and with charm.

It is inevitable that most of your communication at work will be done by sending and receiving emails. But now and then, try to pinch yourself and say, 'Wouldn't this be better if I went and *talked to them?*'

What a speed camera can tell you about making friends and influencing people

Of all modern inventions, the roadside speed camera must surely be the most irritating. The sense that Big Brother is watching you is profoundly intrusive. And Big Brother isn't just watching you; he's probably also fining you and putting points on your licence, without your even knowing, until it's too late.

At least the government has the sensitivity to put up warning signs when a speed camera is lurking. Those warning signs aren't merely very helpful: there's also something curiously quaint about them. The camera they depict isn't a modern camera, it's an old-fashioned bellows camera of a type that hasn't been in general use for about three generations. I sometimes wonder how drivers younger than me even know it's meant to be a camera. There must be something in our collective unconscious which says 'camera' even to people who've never seen a camera like that.

There's a similarly quaint iconography on my Mac screen. I'm typing this book on a Mac programme called Pages which is the Mac equivalent of Word. The icon for Pages is an old-fashioned ink bottle with a fountain pen. It's an intriguing social observation that Apple, that most forward-looking of corporations, have chosen such an antique symbol to denote the process of writing.

It somehow suggests that real writing is still best done with pen and ink.

There's a lesson in that. Somewhere between 99 per cent and 100 per cent of the writing we do is *not* done with pen and ink. But that old technique still retains a certain charm, a sense of doing things properly.

Even in the rush of modern life, there are moments when a letter, done by hand, using pen and ink, on good paper, has a particular potency. It seems more considered and more dignified, and it creates a message which carries an unusual degree of intimacy yet authority.

Imagine your company is pitching against others for a new contract. After the presentations, you all send a polite note to your client to thank him for the opportunity to pitch. The others – obviously – send an email. You send a handwritten letter. Which is going to get noticed? Their emails, or your more courteous and personal letter? I rest my case.

I always keep a fountain pen and a bottle of ink in my office, so that I can send a real old-fashioned letter when it feels right. I don't do it often, but when I do I'm sure it carries more weight.

In my case, I suffer from handwriting which is irritatingly illegible, so I cheat. I type the main text of the letter, but I use pen and ink to handwrite 'Dear John' at the start and 'Best Wishes, Roger' at the end. Not quite as good as pure handwritten, but it still has a personal touch, and at least they can read it.

It's not a device you'd want to use often, but it's a charming weapon at the right moment. After all, you don't wear a dinner suit and black tie every time you go out, but you still want a smart dinner suit in your wardrobe when it's needed. The fact that, in email world, old-style handwritten letters are dying out makes them even more distinctive when you send them.

Minutes: should they be a death certificate or a birth certificate?

There's an Elvis Costello song with a lyric describing a secretary who 'takes seconds over minutes'.

If only. In life, as opposed to lyric, people don't take seconds over minutes, they take weeks.

The taking and writing of minutes has become an arcane ritual characterised by a bizarre combination of excessive detail and excessive delay. By the time the minutes have been laboriously drafted, redrafted, approved and circulated, everyone has long since forgotten the meeting they purport to record.

Consider what typically happens in most large corporations whenever there is an important meeting.

First, the minute-taking is delegated to the most junior person in the room. Odd that, isn't it, to give the crucial job of summarising the key decisions to the least senior, rather than the most senior? Worse than that, in many cases, a secretary is brought in to do the minute-taking: thereby putting the responsibility for recording decisions in the hands of someone not even involved in taking those decisions. (Before you dismiss that practice as something which only happens in our stuffier and more traditional organisations, let me tell you that one of our most fashionable left-leaning think tanks does precisely that.)

Second, the minutes are drafted, slowly and thoroughly to record *everything* that was discussed. They are then circulated to make sure that everyone agrees with what they say. The result is that it takes an age to produce the wretched minutes, and by the time they come out everyone has forgotten whether they're right or wrong.

Finally, they are approved at the next formal meeting, typically a board meeting at least a month later. Of course, by then most of the agreed actions should already have been taken. So a record of what we're going to do only gets agreed after we're supposed to have done it – though we probably haven't, since the minutes weren't available to prompt us to action. It's a bit like a restaurant which serves you a meal, and then shows you the menu just as you're leaving.

In short, minutes become an overly-detailed and largely meaningless piece of office bureaucracy with little or no relevance to the cut and thrust of what is going on in the business. They have a life (or death) of their own: they become an end in themselves, not a means to the end of translating decisions into action.

There is another way. And there needs to be, because minutes – done properly – are valuable tools to make things happen.

To make sense of minutes it's important to distinguish between a record of *discussions* and a record of *decisions*. Usually minutes record *what was said*, not *what was decided*. The result is that they have great length but little relevance.

Try standing that on its head and do the precise opposite: simply list what was agreed and ignore all the debate before the decision was taken.

Suddenly you have a document which is five lines not five pages, which can be produced in half an hour not half a month, and – most remarkable of all – is genuinely useful. It tells people quickly and simply what they have to do.

How do you make this miracle happen? It's simple: just follow this common-sense method:

1. **Give the minute-taking job to the Chairman of the meeting. If he is running the conduct of the meeting he should run the output.**

2. **Establish a culture whereby everyone accepts that minutes will only record decisions and never record discussions. It's not what people are used to, but when they've lived it once they'll never go back.**

3. **During the meeting, the Chairman notes down what is agreed. It's not an arduous task – most long meetings only produce a handful of real decisions.**

4. The Chairman's list of decisions for action needs to show not just the action agreed, but *who* has the responsibility for getting it done and *when* it will be done by.

5. At the end of the meeting the Chairman reads out his list of decisions, the name of the person responsible for action, and the deadline. So everyone has the chance to accept or challenge. This prevents different people leaving the same meeting with different ideas of what was decided. And it saves time, because . . .

6. The minutes are typed and circulated instantly.

Suddenly minutes are transformed from a document for archive into a document for action. They are no longer a death certificate, describing what has happened when it's all too late; they've become a birth certificate, defining the start of new things.

And you'll have a better business as a result.

There's a postscript to this: what happens if a meeting produces *no decisions?*

The answer is simple: the minutes simply record the fact that the meeting took place, but no decisions were taken. That only has to happen once for everyone involved to be very certain it won't happen twice.

Meetings:
Why? And how?

Meetings present a curious paradox. They ought to be the shared moment when information is discussed, when ideas are debated, and when great plans are formed. Yet all too often I leave a meeting feeling two hours older and not a jot wiser. What's gone wrong?

The truth is that managing a group dynamic is harder than it seems. And it's made worse by the fact that all too often we lurch into meetings with very little forethought about how to make the encounter a constructive one.

Like most aspects of office life, meetings benefit from a bit of preplanning and a healthy dose of common sense.

How you handle a meeting depends on whether you're chairing it or you're simply one of the attendees. Chairing a meeting is much the easier task, because you start with a good degree of control. If you're the one in the chair, there are three tasks you have to concentrate on.

First, be clear in your mind *before the meeting* what you want to get out of it. Meetings which finish badly are always meetings which start badly – in the sense that the person in charge wasn't clear from the outset about the outcome they wanted. It helps to write your thoughts down first, and to debate your hopes and fears about the meeting in advance with one of the other people who'll be at the meeting. What you do before you meet determines much of what happens when you meet.

Second, start the meeting by spelling out quickly what ground you want to cover, what result you hope for, and how long you want the meeting to last. (But if you say you're going to get it done in an hour, you have to keep that promise.)

Lastly, run the meeting in a way that allows everyone to say a bit and no one (importantly, that includes you) to say too much. That's easy to prescribe, but hard to do. You have to run the meeting like a series of conversations, not a series of short lectures. Encourage the shy ones to speak up by asking them directly to give their view. Keep the opinionated ones in line by saying, 'That's an interesting point. What do the rest of you feel about that?' By pushing it back from the individual to the group, you can cut the talkative ones short without putting them down. And if your tone is warm and enthusiastic it makes it much easier to control the others.

One final thought on chairing: turn your mobile off when you start and, as you do so, politely ask everyone else to do the same. There is nothing which undermines the dynamic of a meeting more than someone fiddling with their mobile when someone else is trying to make a point. It's a simple courtesy you observe in the cinema, so observe it in the office too.

If you think running a meeting is hard, being one of the attendees is a lot harder. You can't steer the car from the back seat, so you're utterly dependent on the chair to keep things moving. You won't always be lucky: I get bored quickly, and I have been in too many meetings where I really felt I'd lost the will to live. But the same principle applies for an attendee as it does for the chair – you'll get more out of the meeting if you plan in advance. What outcome do you want? And how can you get it?

Once you're clear about what you want, it often helps to talk to someone else before the meeting and see if you can get them on your side. It's much better to win the argument before it has begun.

When you're in the meeting, remember that a meeting is a kind of interview in disguise. You're being judged by the way you perform.

So interview disciplines apply: radiate interest and enthusiasm, keep your comments crisp and clear, and remind yourself that you need to be a good listener as well as a good talker.

It's shrewd politics to be seen to be a good listener. And if you listen to the debate intelligently, you can come in at the end with an opinion which is really a summary of everyone else's good ideas, but will make it seem like you're the one with the right answer.

A good technique to avoid being disappointed by meetings is not to expect too much in the first place. After all, a meeting is simply a committee by another name – and bitter experience teaches us how little committees usually achieve. Often the best route is to regard the meeting itself as an opportunity to demonstrate your ability to be a team player, and to get the decision you want by lobbying the key people outside the meeting.

How to be sure a project will fail

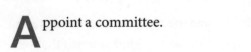

Appoint a committee.

How to be sure a project will succeed

You may feel a bit short-changed by the last chapter, as it was so ridiculously brief.

In truth, I was influenced by two things. First, I rather hoped that I might get into *Guinness World Records* as the writer of the shortest chapter in literature. Just three words will be hard to beat. Second, I really do believe that committees are the kiss of death if you want to get anything done.

But to be a little more constructive, why don't committees work, and how can you manage projects to get a good result?

The answer lies in the psychology of how we all behave when faced with a task. If we share the responsibility for the task with others, we understandably feel that the commitment to getting things done lies with the team, not with one individual. So our personal commitment is inevitably diluted. Subconsciously, we imagine that someone else on the team is really going to drive the project. Trouble is, everyone else thinks that too: the result is that no one gets hold of the challenge. We all wait around for someone else to get things started.

But if the responsibility lies with one person, there's no room for doubt. If you're that one person, *you* have to do it. There's nowhere to hide: if you have to do it, you will do it.

Why do committees exist then? I think the answer is simply that they make us feel comfortable. We are reassured by the notion that lots of people involved means lots of talent involved, so the job will be done well. But in reality, the job won't be done at all. You may think I'm being cynical, but can you think of a project in your experience which has been successfully launched by a committee? The composer Sibelius famously said that no one ever erected a statue to a critic. Maybe it's time to add that no one ever erected a statue to a committee either.

The classic example of the ineffectual nature of committees is the nonsense we call 'brainstorming'. This practice consists of getting a large group of people together to solve a problem, and letting their discussion roam off in any and every direction, in the risible belief that suddenly a moment of brilliance will unveil itself. This daft practice owes its existence not to its effectiveness (it has none), but to the warm feeling we have in a group – we are freed of responsibility because we imagine someone else will find the answer.

But if you want an answer to a difficult problem, you don't want people feeling warm and comfortable. You want them feeling that chill of fear anyone has when it's down to them and no one else. The smaller the group, the greater the chill, because there are fewer people to share the responsibility with. And the smallest group is a group of one. If you're on your own, you *must* make it happen, so the adrenaline flows. And it *does* happen.

Give a job to one person, and you've made them accountable. So they will deliver for you.

But how do you know who is the right person?

Start by writing down the kind of talents your ideal leader will have. Does the job need creativity, forcefulness, attention to detail, a big vision? Don't make a great long list – you'll never find someone to meet the task. Just identify the two or three characteristics that really matter.

When you do this, concentrate on the temperament you need, not the experience. The fact that someone has done something similar before is reassuring, but doesn't prove they have the right mindset. In fact, often the opposite is the case: if you give the job to some-one who's already done something similar they are likely to give you a reheated version of their previous answer. But give it to someone who has never handled that kind of problem and they'll be forced to think things through from first principles, so you're much more likely to get fresh thinking and an original answer.

I was once asked to chair a travel company that sold packaged hol-idays to Italy; their holidays were good quality and their customers were happy. But they hadn't made a profit in twenty years. The board resented my arrival as I had never worked in the travel trade before and I didn't know anything about it. (I did point out to them that being an expert wasn't much use either, since they were all highly experienced and yet the business carried on losing money.)

It was quickly obvious that when the company chartered a plane to take their customers to Italy, they were taking the risk that they could sell most of the seats in the plane. If they didn't, and then had to fly the plane with too many empty seats that still had to be paid for, they'd lose money.

85

I suggested that they did a deal with the airline to buy the seats on a sale or return basis, so they'd only have to pay for the seats they actually used. They all laughed, and then explained that you couldn't do that – it wasn't how the travel trade worked. I replied that their bit of the travel trade wasn't working anyway, since they were losing money; they had no alternative but to find a different way of doing things.

It took me an age to persuade them to think differently, but eventually they went to the airline and explained that they had to work with them in a new way, otherwise they'd go bust and the airline would lose them as a customer – and we showed them our books to prove that we weren't bluffing.

Faced with the choice of giving us a better deal or seeing us disappear, the airline started to sell us tickets on sale or return, and we started making a profit almost immediately.

The reason I came up with a solution was because *I didn't understand the business* – so I didn't know what conventional wisdom said you couldn't do. It taught me that not knowing can often be more useful than knowing – it forces you back to basics, whereas people in the know often can't spot the obvious.

So when you choose your project leader, go for the relevant temperament not the relevant experience. A leader with no knowledge but bags of determination will give you a better answer than someone with enough knowledge but not enough passion.

What happens once you've chosen your leader?

You need to give the leader just three things.

First, state a clear vision of what you want him to achieve. Don't tell him how to do it – that's for him to decide. But be clear about what you want him to get done. He can decide the route and the method of travel: you must be clear about the destination. A good way of doing this is to answer the question, 'What will success look like?'

Second, give him a deadline. If you don't stipulate when a job must be finished, it won't ever be finished.

Third, give him the confidence to do the job well. Say why he, in particular, was chosen for the task and make him feel good about the talents he has and which you want brought to bear. *Above all, make it clear that he – and nobody else – is in charge of this and responsible for a good result.*

If you get this right, they'll walk out of your office feeling proud of themselves, excited about the opportunity, and a healthy bit fearful that they must deliver.

I was pretty sneering about committees earlier on. And I stick with that: if you want action as well as discussion, give the responsibility to one person. That doesn't mean there's no value in meeting as a group. It gives you the opportunity to debate and explore different ways of dealing with a problem. It also gives everyone the chance to know what everyone else is doing. So committees can be a useful part of the process. But they don't work as a way of making decisions. Ultimately, the leader has to decide.

Democracy is fine in politics, but in work life you need a bit of benign dictatorship if you're going to get anything done. That's why you must put one person in charge.

Publish and be damned – or how to deal with journalists

Any successful business career will, sooner or later, bring you in touch with journalists. Most people instinctively fight shy of this moment, but they shouldn't. Like it or not, journalists are a central part of business life and you won't form a good relationship with them by avoiding them.

'Know the enemy' is a good maxim for warfare, and it's a good maxim for business too. So it's worth understanding why journalists seem threatening, and what makes them tick.

Put simply, problems with journalists come in two forms: first, they know something you don't want them to know, and second, you know something you *do* want them to know.

Faced with problem number one, the usual response is to deny the story and/or to threaten the journalist. Therein lies disaster. Journalists are well used to being threatened, with anything from a call to their editor to a full-blown lawsuit. They are not afraid of either: their experience tells them that people threaten most when their position is weakest. Getting cross with a journalist suggests that you are on the defensive, which in turn suggests that the story is true. At any rate, shouting at people usually produces an equal and opposite reaction to the one intended and undermines any hope you have of getting a sympathetic story.

No, if a journalist has a story you don't want them to print, just accept that the reason you don't want it printed is not just because it's damaging, it's also because it's true. So don't deny it. Accept it, and then deal with it.

But what does that mean in practice?

To answer that, stop thinking about the issue from your point of view and start thinking about it from the journalist's point of view. He has a story – and writing stories is how he earns his keep. So he's going to write the story, whatever you say. But he's probably got it from only one source, and he may well not have the whole picture. He's going to respond warmly to anyone in the know (and that could be you) who is willing to share that knowledge, so he can write a fuller, better story.

Avoid your instinct to say *as little as possible*: replace it with an urge to say *as much as possible*. Every business leader I've met who gets good PR is also astutely but splendidly indiscreet.

This candour is exactly what the journalist needs – and what he very rarely gets from cautious business folk. Which makes it so refreshing when it happens. Willingness to be open with a journalist is a much more potent weapon than you might imagine.

And you can put safe boundaries on your openness. If there's something you want to say but don't want to see in print, make it clear that you want it 'off the record' (which means he can use it as background, but not quote it) or 'unattributable' (which means he can use the quote, but can't say it came from you). Contrary to what you might expect, 99 per cent of journalists respect this convention honourably. After all, they know that if they lose your trust once, you will never help them again.

You've already built a bridge with the journalist: you're open and you're helpful, unlike almost all of your peers. Now you can use that bridge. Don't deny bad news – that just makes you look foolishly defensive. But put the bad news in context. As an example, you're not firing staff because the business is in trouble, you're firing staff as part of a cost-saving drive in the light of a tough economy.

While we're on that subject, speak in English not business gobbledygook: if you're firing people, say you're firing people, don't say 'downsizing'. A journalist's first skill is with words, so he can see through euphemistic jargon at fifty paces. Even more offensive than 'downsizing' is 'letting people go' ... Most people in employment are not straining at the leash to be out of work. Tell the truth, even the painful truth, as it is, and you'll be respected for it.

Then link the bad news with some good. Maybe you're firing people in London, but you have just taken on some bright new talent in Manchester. It's up to you to find the ray of sunshine, but at any time in the life of a business there are good things and bad things happening together – you just need to look around to spot the good stuff. It doesn't have to be relevant to the story, as long as positive can act as a counter-balance to negative.

I once had some bad profit figures for a UK-based business to announce. But we had also won a big order in Japan. I briefed the journalist on both points, stressing that we were nervous about the UK economy and saw Asia as an opportunity for growth. We got a very favourable story about our strategy of expansion in Asia, and the bad profits were buried somewhere in paragraph three.

It's vital in all of this to move fast. A journalist might easily ring you about a difficult story at four in the afternoon, with a plan to write his story in the following hour or so, for a six o'clock deadline. If he hasn't got your side of the story by six, the story will appear anyway, and your view will never be known. Business timetables run over weeks, but journalists' timetables run over hours. It's no good being clever after the paper is printed. So, understand this, be brave enough to drop what you're doing and deal with the press instantly. Otherwise, you won't deal with them at all.

In short, be quick, be open, accept the negatives, but give them a positive framework. You won't get a perfect story, but that was never going to happen anyway. But you will get the best you can.

The next step is to think through who's going to be upset by the story – maybe your boss, maybe shareholders – and prepare them for it. If they know in advance that something unflattering in the press is on its way, they'll feel involved and they'll be fore-warned. It's surprising how often the actual story is less alarming than the expectation, and you'll be congratulated for a good result.

So it's really very simple. When a journalist has a story you don't want them to have, you just need to do three things. First, recognise that the story will appear, with or without your cooperation. It's better that it appears with your cooperation, so don't hinder the journalist, help him. Second, find some positives to sweeten the negatives. And third, give clear advance warning that a bad story is on its way. Chances are that the real event will be much less painful than the expectation.

You've learnt how to handle bad news: but can you handle good news?

We've looked at how to handle a journalist when they have a bad news story, but what about the other task – the time when you have a positive story that you want to see in print?

Paradoxically, this can be more difficult than you expect. Much more difficult. That's because we always imagine that our good news is hugely interesting to the rest of the world, and journalists are wise enough to know that's not the case. A journalist's self-respect, and the respect of his peers, hinges on only pushing stories that have some meat on the bone, stories that will really matter to a wider world.

Just as part of your morning is spent deleting emails from people trying to sell you something you don't want, so a journalist spends a few moments of their morning tossing half-read press releases into the bin – simply because the stories are not remarkable enough.

So if you want your story to appear, what should you do?

Begin by being self-critical: is this story genuinely of interest to others? If it isn't, how can it be developed so it starts to have momentum?

An effective but rarely used way of resolving this is to ring up a friendly journalist and ask them. If they think the story lacks something, what would change their view? Maybe some bare news would be more enticing if you could offer an interview with someone involved in the story. Or maybe the content of the story needs to be shaped to give it a genuine point of difference.

Do all that you can to give your story some real edge. And remember that a newspaper is a visual as well as a verbal medium. A great photo or a strong idea which leads to a bold headline will get a journalist's attention in a way that swathes of detailed text never will.

Please note that I referred a moment ago to 'a friendly journalist'. Most people in business only talk to journalists when they absolutely have to. So when they need help, they have no continuing relationship to generate that help. It's crucial for you to take the time and the trouble to meet journalists, and get to know them when you are not after something. Then, when you are, they're much more likely to be there for you. Buy them lunch, cultivate them, invite them to events. Above all, give them any bits of news you've heard. That news doesn't have to be about your business; a journalist starts every day with several blank pages to fill, and he wants to hear everything that's going on.

And never forget that he practises a trade which makes most people feel suspicious and threatened – so treating a journalist like a normal human being will be more welcome than you might expect.

So you've built some friendships, and you've got a story you think is strong enough to command attention. You've sharpened the story so it's bold and simple. You've even got a good photo to bring it to life. Now what?

Start by choosing the one journalist you think will give you the best hearing. That's partly a judgement about how you get on with the journalist, partly a judgement about which paper is most likely to welcome the story, but it's mostly a judgement about which paper you'd like to be in.

Note: we're talking about *one* paper, not more. Journalists are obsessed with the idea of getting exclusive stories. Immortalised in Evelyn Waugh's archaic, but still hilarious, novel *Scoop*, this obsession makes journalists value a story more than they should as long as they have it to themselves. So choose one paper; offer an exclusive; and, if they don't bite, offer it – still as an exclusive – to your next choice.

When you've chosen your journalist, how do you serve up the story? Not, repeat not, with a press release. The press release is the devalued currency of journalism. They are what a newspaper's wastepaper baskets are lined with.

But you should still write a kind of press release – a written summary of the main points of your story will help you get your thoughts clear. But don't send it. Do your briefing verbally. Ideally, go to see the journalist and do it face to face. Failing that, brief them on the phone. Never do it by email or press release – you need human contact to get a good result.

When you've done the verbal briefing, you can then offer to send the release as an aide-memoire for the journalist. But even when you do send it, don't head it 'Press Release'. Head it 'Confidential, for (name of selected journalist)'. That confirms your contact is getting an exclusive.

Be warned: a story isn't a story without quotes and a photo. That means your release must include a couple of good quotes and must be supported by a good photo. So be prepared. Get a photo organised in advance; and do it well. Book a good photographer who can make something of the opportunity. It'll cost a bit more in planning, time and money, but the photo is much more likely to be used. And then draft a quote or two. These should not be in some dead corporate-speak that sounds like footnotes from the annual report and accounts: they should be fresh, straightforward and human. That way, there's a reasonable chance they'll appear in print.

And even a reasonable chance you'll be glad they did.

When you're responding to a bad story, you must be ready to move fast. But when you're creating a good story, you have time on your side. So use it. Get the story crisp, get good quotes crafted, and get a good photo in place. Then you can pounce.

The one common element between damage limitation on a bad story and opportunity creation on a good story is that you need an honest, human relationship with your journalist. To most of us, journalists appear at the bottom of the social pecking order, down with politicians and traffic wardens, well below estate agents and rat-catchers. If you're the one who deals with them warmly and openly, they'll reciprocate more often than you expect.

Why the right answer
isn't the right answer

Y ou could be forgiven for thinking, naively, that once you've solved a problem in the office, then you've solved it.

If only. The painful reality is that solving a problem is only halfway to the answer. Because once you've solved it, you've still got to get other people to believe in it, the same way you do. It's no use *having the idea* if you can't *sell the idea*.

So, how do you sell your idea; how do you get people on your side?

If you need to pitch an idea to someone, start by giving yourself generous time to plan your pitch. The need to plan your big moves is a recurring theme of this book, and I don't apologise for that. Nothing of value happens in life without other people's cooperation; and you're much more likely to get them to do what you want them to do if you first dedicate time to plotting how that can be achieved. You wouldn't go on a journey to a strange place without first having a long, hard look at the map – yet I'm continually amazed by the way people at work often have strong ambitions, but give themselves no time to plan how these ambitions might be made real.

When you're making your plan, put your own hopes and fears to one side: instead try to get inside the mind of the person you need to persuade. Understand their agenda. Politically, are they more concerned with what their boss thinks than what is the right thing to do? Emotionally, are they innately more cautious than most?

Then, try to define the positives that will appeal to your audience, and try to define the negatives that may scare them. Personalise the positives: articulate those positives in terms that will be relevant to them, not you. Could your idea help their career, or ease their workload? Next, anticipate the negatives, and look for ways to defuse them. If cost is going to be a worry, can it be covered within an existing budget, or are there savings elsewhere that can compensate?

Never forget that people behave as if they are driven by logic, but, in truth, emotion is a much more powerful motivator. Presenting your case so that it's justified logically is all very well, but what will win the argument for you is to get your audience on your side *emotionally*. Think through not just what they'll *think* about your idea, but what they'll *feel* about it.

When you present your case, keep it simple. If someone is trying to sell an idea, there's a terrible tendency for them to put forward every possible supporting argument, backed up by every available fact and figure. They fondly imagine that, by being thorough, they're more likely to win the day.

In reality, the opposite is true. Too many strands of argument become indigestible, and start to cancel each other out. What the speaker thinks is a wonderfully comprehensive case becomes, to the listener, plain boring.

Strip down your case to the bare essentials. Being thorough may make us feel comfortable, but it can be dull for the decision-maker.

It hardly needs saying that boring your audience won't help your cause. I can't imagine anyone saying, after a pitch, 'That guy went on too long and was frightfully tedious – so let's give him our support.'

A clever technique is to try to make your audience feel that they have some ownership of your proposal. Don't say, 'I've got this great idea ... ' Already, your audience is on the defensive, feeling as if they are on the receiving end of a sales call.

Instead, say, 'I'd like your advice on this ... ' Now your audience feel involved, and if they end up thinking it was them, not you, who invented the plan, they're much more likely to approve it.

It's worth working at all this. How you pitch yourself and your ideas is crucial to success, not just at work but in life. It's so important, I could write a book about it. In fact, I already have. Co-written with the brilliant Stephen Bayley, it's called *Life's a Pitch* and if you're ambitious you should read it. There's a story in it which encapsulates marvellously what I've just been saying. It describes how Gerry Robinson, already a huge success in business, was persuaded by Tony Blair's government to take on the chairmanship of The Arts Council, with a view to using his tough business skills to slash their budget.

But when Gerry got stuck into the job, he realised that spending on the arts was a worthwhile investment not a waste, and that the budget should be *increased*, not cut. That was a hard sell to the government that had put him in the post to do the opposite. So he went to see Tony Blair and his tight-fisted chancellor, Gordon Brown.

He simply said to Blair that, 'Every civilised country funds its arts properly.'

Brilliant. No spreadsheets and analyses. Just a powerful appeal direct to Blair's vanity. Every prime minister wants to see his country in the civilised group, not the third-world also-rans.

Then he said to Brown, 'It's a tiny amount of money we need. Only about £200 million – that's barely the cost of one F11 fighter jet.'

Brilliant again. You and I think £200 million is a lot. But expressed that way, it seems trifling to argue over it.

This story demonstrates my themes beautifully. Gerry had understood the motivations of his audience perfectly, had concentrated on the emotional over the logical, and presented his case with utter simplicity.

I hardly need add that he got the money.

Would you mind saying that in English please?

If you have the fortune and misfortune to be English, as I am, there are several things to grumble about. Our football teams have a habit of nearly being successful, but never quite getting there; our weather is predominantly grey; and if you get good service in an English restaurant it's because the person serving you comes from Bordeaux not Bridlington.

But there is one great thing we English *do* have – a magnificent language, which is textured and expressive like no other. England has produced few world-class painters (after Turner you're struggling), but our literature is unparalleled: Shakespeare, Milton, Donne, Keats, Shelley, Wordsworth, Dickens, Austen – you could go on for ever. But that's no surprise: they all had such wonderful raw material to work with. The English language is not only envied by the rest of the world, it's increasingly being used by the rest of the world. It has become the international language of business, of travel, of diplomacy.

Yet, blessed with this amazing natural resource, we often use it with astonishing clumsiness – especially in business life. Instead of communicating in plain, clear English, we lapse into a terrible business speak, riddled with jargon and clichés. We never have good old-fashioned problems; now we have 'issues'. Nothing is ever hard – it's 'challenging'. Nothing seems to be a nightmare – now it's a 'nightmare scenario'. (The first person to explain the difference gets a free bottle of champagne from me.) We don't think, we 'strategise'. And so on.

Jargon is, essentially, a specialised language for a particular activity, and it has its place. I'm keen on sailing, and I used to race a small yacht. I once counted: on my boat there are fifteen different terms for a rope. People who don't sail are mystified by 'sheets' and 'guys' and 'halyards' and 'cunninghams' and 'outhauls' – all of them different types of rope. They assume that these terms exist mainly to make non-sailors feel inadequate. But they'd be wrong: the reason that my boat had fifteen different terms for a rope is that the ropes in question had fifteen different functions. If you're racing in a stormy sea with an armada of other yachts all converging on the same point, it's vital to issue instructions with total clarity. Distinguishing quickly between one rope and another matters – both for speed and safety.

Similarly, I imagine in an operating theatre there's a mass of jargon to differentiate between all the tools of the trade. The surgeon wants to be able to say one word and know the nurse will hand him exactly the right scalpel for that task. That kind of jargon is genuinely useful. It seems arcane to the layman, but it's quicker and clearer for the expert.

But jargon in business is often not aimed to make things clearer, it seems to be used to hide rather than reveal. Here is a quote from a recent Burberry annual report:

'In the wholesale channel, Burberry exited doors not aligned with brand status and invested in presentation through both enhanced assortments and dedicated customised real estate in key doors.'

While you're laughing at the bizarre mixture of pomposity and meaninglessness offered by that quote, I'd like to thank Lucy Kellaway, a particularly witty and brilliant journalist for bringing this garbage to our attention in her *Financial Times* column.

Now read it again, and ask yourself if you understand what they're trying to say. No, me neither.

I'm glad Burberry has a good grasp of fashion and trench coats. They certainly have no grasp of communication.

But does this really matter? Yes, it does, and here's why. Among any group of people, be it an army at war, a football team in a match, or the managers of a business, success depends significantly on the ability to communicate with each other quickly and clearly.

Think about people in your office who are admired: can they get their message across simply and well? Of course they can. Because they can communicate well about what they are trying to achieve, they are much more likely to achieve it. By the same token, how often have you left a meeting a bit uncertain about what's supposed to happen next? It's a common problem, and where there's no clarity about what's to be done, it doesn't get done.

Strong management and inspiring leadership hinges on being able to say what's happening, and what must be done about it, in simple English we can all understand.

So why do we fall back on clichés and business speak? There are, I believe, three reasons, and it's worth knowing them and their implications.

The first reason someone's communication to others might not be clear is that they themselves are not clear in their own mind about what they want to say. You can't say anything that makes sense to others until you've thought it through properly yourself. So if your message isn't clear, ask yourself if you are truly sure you know what you want, *before* you start asking for it.

Second, business speak is partly driven by cowardice. If we have a huge problem, it takes courage to say so. It's much easier to hide behind a euphemism or two. I once heard a noted investment banker describe a business which was in dreadful financial trouble as 'experiencing sub-optimal performance'. A few months later, the company went bust; the banks lost their money; the shareholders lost their shirts; and thousands of workers lost their jobs. If the banker had the nerve to say the business was in dire straits, rather than 'experiencing sub-optimal performance' maybe we'd have faced up to the problem bravely enough to solve it before it was too late.

It is a disease of modern life that we often speak in language which is designed to conceal the truth, not expose it. The global recession we now face began when banks in the USA started lending extravagantly to people who couldn't remotely afford to pay back the commitments they had taken on. But because the banks wanted the short-term commissions that went with those loans, they did not describe the deals as 'irresponsible' or 'foolhardy', but as 'sub-prime'. By using such euphemistic language, the real level of risk was nicely obfuscated. The loan salesmen got their commission and poor people became homeowners. The only problem was that they quickly moved from homeowner to homeless when they couldn't repay the debt; the banking system spiraled out of control; and capitalism came as close to the brink as it has ever been.

Lastly, it's assumed that business speak sounds important. I imagine that whoever drafted that absurd Burberry statement about '... dedicated customised real estate in key doors' thought this inflated tone made the Burberry position look somehow more serious. But it doesn't: it makes Burberry look stupid. Sensible people can see through pomposity at fifty paces.

The truth is that the communication which inspires confidence is not grandiloquent, it's refreshingly simple. People respect leadership which is clear, not complicated.

But that kind of crisp communication isn't easy to achieve – you have to work at it. And to work at it successfully, you need to follow some guidelines.

To start with, be sure that your own train of thought is clear. Write down the important things you want to say, just as simple bullet points, before you develop that into a memo or a talk. If you have defined the basic content in the simplest and barest way first, then everything else falls into place.

Next, spend time on what you want to say: rethink, revise, and simplify all the time. In the office, when I want to get a statement done quickly, I often dictate it in draft to my secretary, then I work on the draft to see what needs to be added to complete it. But I always discover that I am not adding, but taking away. The message gets clearer the more it gets distilled.

Finally, be honest. That may seem obvious, but a constant weakness in office communication is that everyone's instinct is always to play down problems. It's easy to see why – we fear the painful truth. But the result of minimising problems is that they don't get dealt with. It's a bit like going to the doctor, but not telling them all the symptoms because you're frightened of discovering that you've got some ghastly disease. Trouble is, the doctor can't cure you until they know what you're suffering from. It's the same in the office: if you hide from problems, they don't get dealt with, they fester.

The irony is that people at work hide from painful truths, but you can win real respect by being the one who is brave enough to confront them. Folk aren't stupid, and they know those problems are there. So they'll be inspired by someone who deals with them openly.

A vivid example of this comes from Winston Churchill, one of the greatest (and clearest) orators of recent history. On taking office as prime minister in the dark days at the start of World War II, he gloomily announced, 'I have nothing to offer but blood, toil, tears and sweat.'

Instantly, the whole nation understood they had a leader who knew the truth and wasn't frightened of it. So began a leadership which turned the tide of history. Just eleven words: short, simple, truthful and brave. We can learn from that.

HOW TO DEAL WITH **YOURSELF**

Which would you rather have – a mission statement or a mission?

Beware – this question isn't quite as simple or naive as it looks. You would, of course, imagine that any company which had a mission would have crystallised that in a mission statement. Equally, you'd reasonably assume that any company which had a mission statement would, by definition, have a mission. But you'd be wrong: it constantly amazes me that businesses which do have a sense of mission generally don't have a mission statement, and businesses with a mission statement proudly hanging on the wall often seem to be run with little sense of mission.

What's going on here? To answer that, let's understand what we mean by 'mission statement' and 'mission'. A mission is, in this context, a sense of purpose, a driving ambition. A mission statement is a written corporate policy, sometimes in the company's literature or on their website, which aims to distil in a few words that sense of purpose, that ambition.

Fine – but what's the big distinction between the two terms? The answer is that a statement is just words, but a mission is something in the company's DNA, something in the bloodstream. And that starts to point to the underlying problem: a company with a statement is making a promise, but a company with a mission is delivering that promise. It's the difference between talking about it and doing it.

You may ask at this point, does this really matter to me, isn't this all a problem for the Chief Executive?

It does matter to you. First, I'm assuming that if you're reading this book you're planning to be a Chief Executive one day. You might as well be prepared.

Second, a sense of mission doesn't live just on the executive floor; it's part of the life and culture of the whole business, and everyone has a part to play in shaping and growing that culture. Including you.

But why do companies frequently publish a mission statement, but not follow it? The culprits are usually large corporations which, as they have grown, have got complacent, and started to lose their sense of direction. They sense this and try to correct their slippage by defining – or to be more accurate, by redefining – what they are trying to achieve. The problem is that by then it's a lost cause.

Companies start to worry about their mission statement when they are at that point in their corporate life cycle when passion has been replaced by bureaucracy. So the mission statement they write is not charged with purpose; it's charged with compromise. They try to promise to be all things to all people. They aim to do the best for their shareholders, their staff, their customers, their suppliers – and probably the couple who run the pub round the corner.

Many large companies have mission statements with an unintentionally comic quality. They are so eager to promise everything to everyone that they end up saying nothing. My wife is a left-wing English teacher in a state school, but she also has a few shares given to her by her father. (When I accused her of being a champagne socialist, she said, 'Yes, it's the best type of socialist to be.') She is not that interested in business, but she once came up with a very astute observation: if you go into a corporation's office and see their mission statement framed on the wall, that's the time to sell your shares in that company.

What she was observing was the same point about a company's life cycle that I made: a company starts to publish mission statements when it's running out of energy. The mission statement becomes a document of defence, not a plan of attack.

When a company's arteries are hardening, it tends to spend a lot of time discussing and writing about where it needs to go, but spends very little time actually going there. A company which has lost its sense of direction uses a mission statement to post-rationalise its position, to justify the status quo, rather than to define a clear new future.

The reason that so many mission statements sound so fluffy is that they are all statement and no mission.

What about businesses that do have a real sense of purpose? Why don't they capture it in a mission statement? Of course they should, but usually they are too busy living their ambitions to want to write them down. I've worked with Terence Conran for several years, and his sense of purpose is very clear – but he spends his energy pursuing his aims, not producing documents about them. Terence has an extraordinary sense of theatre, so when he designs a restaurant, for instance, it becomes more than a place to eat food, it becomes an experience. His mission is to design things not as objects but as experiences. We did eventually define our mission in those terms, but it was as a sales tool to describe our business to potential customers, not as an internal statement to guide our own staff. They knew it instinctively anyway.

This is not to suggest – assuming you have a clear mission – that you shouldn't write a statement. Entrepreneurial types often don't, but that doesn't mean they're right, it just means they underestimate the value of spelling out what they want to achieve. If you have a mission, you should define it. It will help you raise money for the business if it's new; it'll help you recruit good people; it'll help you win customers; and above all it'll help you keep your eyes on the target.

Just make sure it's a mission statement with a mission: it must be clear, crisp, to the point. The simpler your mission statement is, the more likely you are to achieve that mission.

Done is better than perfect

This five-word rubric was a favourite saying of an extraordinary and famous man.

If you've read his intriguing biography, you'll already know which famous man. But if you haven't, you may be surprised to know that the man in question was Steve Jobs.

Anyone who has scrolled across the touch screen of an iPad, or tapped the keys of a MacBook, will know that much of the charm of Apple's remarkable products is their sense of perfectionism. The designs are perfectionist in their beauty, and the detail of how they work seems perfectionist too. So why is Steve Jobs – the genius who made Apple what it is – apparently relegating 'perfect' to second place in his priorities?

When Jobs said 'done is better than perfect' (as he often did) I do not believe that he did not want perfect products. What he meant was that he did not want the search for a perfect answer to become an endless quest that stopped the job ever being finished. And this shows that Jobs was a shrewd psychologist as well as a brilliant entrepreneur.

He realised that people are often frightened of completing a job: completion means commitment, and to commit yourself is to make a decision. We are often frightened of making a decision, because then we can be judged. If we postpone the decision, we postpone the judgement. There seems no better way of postponing a decision than saying, 'it's good but it's not yet perfect'.

This view overlooks something important. Of course, if we commit to a course we can then be judged to be right or to be wrong. But if we don't commit, we can still be judged: not as right or wrong, but as indecisive. And to be indecisive is a much bigger crime than to be wrong from time to time.

In the office I'm fond of declaring that a bad decision on Monday makes more money than a good decision on Friday.

A big part of your job in the office, whatever that job is, is about getting stuff done.

You have to get on with things, to make decisions. Sometimes you'll be right, sometimes not. But you're moving things forward. People at work respect someone who is decisive, even if the decision isn't always perfect. They recognise that leadership is about pushing on, making things happen. By contrast, no decision means no action. And if you don't take action, why bother to go to work at all?

This is not an argument in favour of being impulsive. Some decisions (usually small ones) are best taken quite impulsively. Life is short and if there's not much at stake either way, you might just as well decide now as later. Equally, decisions where the implications are bigger need some real thought first. But that pause for thought must be a means to an end, not an end in itself.

'Think then decide' is good. 'Think instead of deciding' is far from good.

Twice in my business life I've fired someone for being chronically indecisive. In each case, the victim of my frustration asked me what they'd done wrong. In each case, my reply was simple: 'You haven't done anything wrong. The problem is that you haven't done *anything*. Right or wrong.'

There's a great term which HR people often use: it's to describe someone as a good 'completer/finisher'. There is a personality type that has an instinct for finishing things, for getting tasks completed. But it's a talent which is more rare than we'd care to admit. Yet that talent is something we all have to learn.

As Steve Jobs knew only too well.

The joy of laziness

It's widely assumed that high achievers tend to be hard workers. I suspect that's often the case – yet the truth is that many low achievers are hard workers too. And the number of low achievers out there greatly outnumbers the high achievers.

When we say that high achievers tend to be hard workers, there's an implication that it's the hard work which created the high achievement. I think it happens the other way round: the kind of people who are driven to be high achievers are driven to be hard workers too. They're not high achievers because they're hard workers, they're hard workers because they're high achievers.

The equation between hard work and good results isn't as simple as it appears at first sight, and that's why plenty of low achievers are hard workers too.

At any rate, what do we mean by hard work? Do we just mean long hours at the desk? Shouldn't we be thinking more about the concept of *good* work rather than *hard* work? In other words, I'm suggesting that good work is more a function of quality than quantity. We can all remember days at the office when we stayed late and yet didn't really accomplish quite what we hoped, and we can remember other days when it all seemed to flow productively, and everything happened quickly.

We need to stop thinking about long hours and start thinking about useful hours. In fact I'm convinced that long hours can often make it harder to solve a problem, not easier. There's a good adage that you should never do something important if you're angry or if you're tired. It's wise advice; and if you work excessively long hours you may or may not be angry, but you'll certainly be tired. Then your work rate slows down, and the quality of your work tends to slide too. So what you were doing takes longer and the results will be less good.

I get impatient with people who think that because they've worked a long day they've therefore worked a productive day.

Working *well*, as opposed to working *hard*, means feeling fresh and bringing a clear head to the task. Sir Gerry Robinson, one of Britain's shrewdest (and richest) businessmen was obsessed with this. He never came to the office before about 9.30 a.m., he never stayed later than about 5.00 p.m., and he never took work home in the evening or at weekends. On top of that, he enjoyed good holidays. He broke his own rule rarely, for an important evening meeting, or during a crisis like a big takeover. But 98 per cent of the time he worked to a very relaxed and unpressured routine. That was much more than a personal preference: he had an almost fetishistic belief that if you work long hours you get stale, you get too close to the problem to see it clearly, and you end up making bad choices.

The result of his apparently almost lazy regime was startling. He was always calm, always charming, always unflustered. When he was working on a project with you, his attention on you and your project would be utterly undivided. He was not only a joy to work for – he also made extremely good decisions.

Cynics may say, 'Well Gerry was the boss, it was easy for him – he had lots of good people around him.'

But the question is: how did he get to be the boss in the first place? And the answer is that he made good decisions on the way up as well as good decisions at the top. He firmly believed that he made those good calls because he was relaxed, so his mind was clear. Of course, he's a very bright man anyway, but I worked closely with him for a decade, and I'm sure that his freshness, and the clarity that went with it, made a big difference.

When I talk to people about the value of pacing their work so they don't get stale, they normally agree enthusiastically about the principle. Then they go on quickly to explain how in practice this couldn't possibly work for them – they just have much too much to do, rushed off their feet, blah, blah, blah.

The truth is that these folk aren't overworked, they're under-organised. Anyone can learn the joy of being a bit more relaxed, a bit more detached, if they put their mind to it.

To start, it's crucial to grasp that long hours are not a sign of ambition, they're a sign of anxiety. Workaholics are driven more by guilt than by hope. And don't imagine that long hours will impress the boss: what the boss wants is good results, not midnight oil. (And if your boss is Gerry Robinson, he won't ever know you're working late as he'll have gone home hours ago.)

So you've got to get into the mindset of recognising that long hours are not a sign of dedication but a sign of disorganisation. Then you need to learn how to manage your day better. That starts with simply making a list of all the things you need to do. Then choose the one item on that list which is particularly important. When I say important, I mean that in a strategic sense: something that will really make a difference if you get it right.

People often confuse 'important' with 'urgent'. Urgent simply means that you need to do it quickly, but there are lots of urgent tasks – like paying the gas bill – which are not remotely important in a strategic way. We tend to spend too much time at work just firefighting: dealing with the here and now, but forgetting about the big, long-term problems.

So, you've isolated your most important, most strategic task. Now identify the most unpleasant task on your list of things to do, the one you're really dreading. That's usually the job which never gets done properly, because it keeps getting put off. Which is precisely why you must grasp the nettle, and get it sorted. And when you do, you'll find it strangely motivating.

You've pinpointed both your most strategic task and your most unpleasant. Now just forget about the others. All of them. They'll get done in due course (after all, they're still on your list) but ignore them for now, or else they will get in the way of what really matters.

Now you've got your two most crucial tasks. Choose one of them, just on instinct, and devote your day to that. When you've cracked it, or maybe you're just bored with it, go to the other big task. But don't let your mind wander to any of the other things on your list until you've made real progress on the two big ones. It's common sense: you'll do the important stuff well if you make it your mission to do so, and that means disciplining yourself to let go of everything else for a while.

The reason the workaholic puts in long hours is partly guilt. But it's also a feeling that they've got to get *everything* done. The result is that they take on far too many tasks and none of them get done properly. It's far better to make a success of one task that truly matters. Let the others wait. Their turn will come. And if a minor job gets neglected, does it really matter? It's a small price to pay for the huge benefit of putting all your energy into something strategic.

If the task you've set yourself is proving tough to deal with, don't try harder – try less hard. Stand back from it and cool down. If I'm working on something at the office which just isn't coming right (and we all know that feeling), I just break off for a while. I might go for a walk, or go and read a magazine over a cappuccino in a local cafe. What I don't do is any other work: I'm keeping my mind free – and when I do go back to my desk it usually starts to fall into place.

And if you go home with a work problem still buzzing in your head, resist the temptation to worry over it that night. It's far better to have a glass of wine and an early night. The next day you'll find that the problem is much easier to unlock.

Trying hard is laudable, but sometimes trying less hard produces a better result.

If you don't believe me, maybe you'll be persuaded by Winston Churchill. When asked by a young admirer what the secret of his success was, Churchill replied with characteristic directness, 'Conservation of energy, dear boy. Never stand up when you can sit down; never sit down when you can lie down.'

Speech without words – the power of body language

We'd all agree, very quickly, that the ability to communicate well is essential to success in office life – indeed essential to success anywhere. Yet there is an implicit assumption in this notion that communication is something that largely happens through words. After all, we communicate through talking, through emails, through meetings. These are all words-based activities.

We need to test that idea. Ask yourself this. When is communication between two people at its most sensitive, its most potent, its most intense? Yes, you're right – it's the communication between lovers.

How much of that is verbal? Answer: some of it is, but this most exquisite and emotionally charged communication is largely conducted by signs not words: a sigh, a glance, a gesture, the flutter of eyelashes, the trace of an innuendo-laden smile. Shakespeare, who knew more than most of us about communicating, describes lovers as 'sighing like furnace'. It's an odd simile, but a vivid one. And it accords with our own experience; lovers don't speak with words, they speak with body language.

You may be tempted to dismiss body language as OK for a steamy affair but not very relevant to life in the office. You'd be wrong.

Think how many common epithets hinge on the concept of using the body to express a mood or an idea. When you're in a positive mood, you're 'on the front foot'. When you're relaxed, you're 'laid back'. When you choose to ignore something, you 'turn a blind eye'. You exhort someone who's down to 'keep their chin up'. If you're a bit naive, you're 'wide-eyed'. And when you have to make an unequivocal apology you 'hold your hands up'. (It's a good game: there are dozens more examples I'm sure you can think of.)

All these common phrases demonstrate our instinctive under-standing that our body communicates our feelings with great eloquence, often without a single word being uttered.

People who understand this better than most are gamblers. It's not my specialist subject: I think I'm making a huge gamble when I put a fiver on the second favourite in the Grand National. But there are those who gamble big sums for a living – often as high-stakes poker players.

Now poker depends on guessing correctly whether your opponent is bluffing or telling the truth. And your opponent, knowing this, will work hard to conceal any emotion – hence the term 'poker-faced'. But a good poker player will still have a strong instinct about whether the other guy is bluffing by watching tiny details of his body language. Virtually everyone – when they're lying – has some tiny quirk of body movement. It may be a nervous smile, or a tendency to avoid direct eye contact, or a gesture, like folding your arms. Poker players have a term for this: it's called the 'tell'. That's the unavoidable sign that what you're saying and what you're thinking aren't quite aligned. So your body is talking for you, even when we don't want it to.

Don't think that 'tells' only happen to riverboat gamblers. They happen all the time in office life too. How many times have you seen someone in a meeting looking furtively at a text or an email on their mobile? That's a 'tell' of disinterest if ever I saw one.

You need to learn the poker player's skill – not just to understand other people (though that's helpful too) but to get your own message across.

Let's start with listening. There's an assumption that when we talk about communicating, we're talking about sending out a message. But that's only half of it; communication is a two-way street, and being a good listener is an important skill if you want to get people on your side.

Simply looking clearly at the person who is speaking suggests that you're listening well. If you make a written note from time to time it tells them that they've made an important point, and they'll feel flattered. Don't make written notes endlessly though; it makes your note-taking seem like a routine and is much less powerful than a note made occasionally.

Even tiny details – like shaking someone firmly by the hand when you greet them – may seem trivial, but they can be strong indicators of confidence. It matters to show that you're at ease with people, not least because it makes it easier for them to feel at ease with you. But being at ease with them isn't everything; the best body language suggests not just that you are at ease with someone but, even more crucially, that you *want to be with them.*

I had a fascinating insight about this from Tim Bell (now Lord Bell) the man who was Chief Executive of the Saatchi and Saatchi advertising agency at the height of its power and who then became Margaret Thatcher's close adviser during her reign as prime minister. Tim, a charmingly impressive man himself, told me that by far the most charismatic man he had ever met was the former US President, Bill Clinton. When I asked why Clinton was so special, Tim's reply was that he had a way of looking at you, which made you feel as if you and he were the only people in the room. He made you feel that you were the one and only person he was interested in.

This is the real key to body language: the ability to make someone else feel valued. It's easy to imagine that someone like Bill Clinton may have that gift (lucky him) and that if you don't, it's too late to try. But that would be a cop-out. Like so much of life, you can get better at it by working at it.

The difficulty with body language is that we're used to considering what we say before we say it, but we're not habituated to planning the signals our body sends out in the same way. It's not instinctive – which is why we need to work at it consciously.

The first step is to stop thinking of yourself as 'you' and start thinking of yourself as 'you, seen through the eyes of other people'. There's a wonderful truism that we are all three people: the person we think we are, the person other people think we are, and the person we really are. Forget one and three and concentrate on number two – the person other people think we are.

The 'you' that matters is the 'you' that others perceive. Put yourself in their place, and then present yourself to them as someone who is genuinely pleased to be with them.

It really doesn't matter if the other person is your boss or the guy getting you a cappuccino in Starbucks: you need to educate yourself to make everyone you're with feel the vibration that you're glad to be with them.

Suddenly every encounter, every relationship seems to be on an easier trajectory. And people will respond to you differently, and more positively. If your body language tells someone that you value being with them, they'll start to value being with you. I can't promise you that you'll emulate Bill Clinton and end up as president of the United States. But I do promise you'll discover that the language of the body can often be more eloquent and more influential than the language of words.

How to become Global Chief Executive by going to the movies more often

We talked in an earlier chapter about the need to avoid the workaholism trap, and the importance of staying fresh if you are going to do good work. That philosophy applies to how you are outside the office as much as it does to how you are in the office.

When you've finished working, it's easy to slump down in front of the television set and do nothing. But the truth is that resting isn't very restful. If you're going to shake off the stress of work and get back on Monday in attack mode, doing *something* is much more relaxing than doing *nothing* – as long as the something is very different from the work you do. Plan your evenings and your weekends so that your mind and your body are being stimulated, not slowed down.

Get physical when you can – go to the gym (mind-numbingly boring in my view, but definitely good for you), play tennis, golf, football, whatever you enjoy. Racing a small sailing boat works best for me – it's physically and intellectually demanding, and not without danger on a windy day. You may say that's stressful, and in a sense it is, but it's a very different kind of stress from worrying about last week's sales figures. Any vigorous outdoor activity is a good antidote to the office.

If you collapse into an armchair at weekends, you'll still feel that work is overwhelmingly important when you return to it on Monday; but if you've done other stuff over the weekend you'll realise that's important too, and it helps put the office in perspective.

There's a widely held view among psychiatrists that physical exercise, be it sport or simply a long walk, helps combat depression. Not every psychiatrist agrees on this, but my own experience tells me that my mind seems fresher when my body has had to work a bit.

It's also vital to exercise your brain a bit outside the office, as well as your body. Go to the theatre, to the cinema, to art galleries, to a lecture. It's thought-provoking and it's enjoyable, *but it's also reminding you that there's a wider world beyond the office.*

We are often asked to 'think outside the box'. This ghastly cliché simply means we must think in a more lateral and creative way. And we certainly need to do that if we are going to solve problems at work. But how can we expect to be more lateral and creative if we don't have much lateral and creative stimulus in our lives? Getting a richer cultural life – more art, more theatre, more books, more debate – generates a mindset which is far better able to find imaginative answers at work.

An evening in an art gallery or at the movies takes you to a very different place from the one you inhabit from nine to six, Monday to Friday. It gets you thinking about very different issues, very different human problems, which, in turn, makes you understand that your problems at work are not that important. Paradoxically, this makes it easier to solve those problems when you return to them. If something is massively important, trying to deal with it can induce a kind of mental paralysis. But if you have it in perspective – you want to get it right, but it's not the end of the world – you'll probably handle it fine.

A good example of this phenomenon is when a professional golfer has to sink a five-foot putt to win a million dollars and a major championship. They often freeze and miss the putt. Yet when they are practising, a championship golfer would sink that putt fifty times out of fifty. Similarly, when a big football match has to be decided on penalties, star players frequently miss, though in practice they'd score every time.

People perform best when they are taking things seriously, but not too seriously. An active life outside work helps achieve that balance.

Inevitably, people of the workaholic mindset often claim that they'd like to do more in the way of galleries, theatre, sport, etc., but they just don't have time.

Nonsense. What they really mean is that they don't have the discipline to find the time. Whenever my wife books tickets for us to go to a movie or a play during the week, I manage to get my work done, and I get to the theatre in time. But if there's nothing in the diary, I slow down a bit at work and finish much later.

If you want a life outside the office, just buy the tickets, put the date in your diary, and it'll happen. If you don't, you'll become a couch potato who knows a lot about what's on TV and little about life.

Bill Shankly, one of the legendary football managers of the past, once said that, 'Some people believe that football is a matter of life and death. I'm very disappointed with that attitude. I can assure you that it's much more important than that.'

It's a great quote, typically Shankly: determined yet witty. Of course, you're not meant to take it seriously, and yet at a certain level, perhaps you are. And that was Shankly's point – to succeed at something, you have to be obsessively committed and yet at the same time you have to be able to keep it in perspective.

Which is why being busy *out* of the office makes you much more effective when you're busy *in* the office.

How to get your boss's job

G etting your boss's job is what we all want isn't it?

No, it's not.

If you want to advance your own career (and I hope you do, otherwise you've bought the wrong book) you need to think about *pushing yourself up*, not *pushing others out of the way*. After all, the person who is most likely to decide your next promotion is your boss, and he's hardly likely to sacrifice his career in order to help yours. You must see your boss as an ally in your ambition, not an obstacle.

So if trying to elbow your boss out of the way is the wrong route to promotion, what is the right route?

Start by being clear about what you want for yourself. Too often people think about promotion in terms of more money. I think that confuses the issue. Real promotion is about more responsibility, not more cash. If you want to grow your career, concentrate on doing more, not on earning more. At any rate, if you do a bigger job, and do it well, more cash will follow.

But while you shouldn't worry too much about the money that goes with promotion, you should worry about the title. I often hear people say titles don't matter – except the people saying that are usually themselves called 'Group Chief Executive' or 'Worldwide Executive Chairman'. The truth is that titles do matter because they define to others what level of responsibility you have. And the reason that the Global Big Boss in Charge of Everything doesn't want to give you a bigger title is that he doesn't want to offend others in the office with lesser titles. But your promotion means nothing unless it's publicly endorsed – which is why you must fight for the title that goes with the job. And when you've got the job, and the title, it needs to be announced to one and all. You can only be sure that the promotion is real when the promotion is public.

But how do we find the path to promotion? There are four tasks you need to set yourself if you are determined to get on.

The first is obvious, but that doesn't mean it's not important. You've got to be effective in your current job. People don't get promoted from a position of weakness, they get promoted from a position of strength. So don't think too much about what you want to do next: think instead about what you're doing now. Work hard at it and do it well.

Second, be liked. This one is much more significant than you might imagine. People who fit in with the team, who get on well with others, are much more likely to be helped up than those who don't. That's partly just human nature's simple tendency to favour the like-able, but it has a more practical edge. Promotions are nice to receive, but they are difficult to award – because they cause jealousy. So it's easier for a boss to promote someone who's liked.

This does not, repeat not, mean that you should rush round *trying* to be liked. In truth there are few things more off-putting than someone behaving like a puppy, craving attention. Instead, just be friendly and positive – and no more than that – with everyone you deal with. Don't be needy, just be warm. And that includes being warm to those below you in the hierarchy. We all tend to suck up to our bosses, but being courteous and interested towards those below you is less instinctive for ambitious types, and sometimes needs a bit of effort. But it gets noticed and it will help to brand you as one of the positive people.

Third, be pushy. Of course you're not likely to be a promotion candidate if you're not doing your current job well. But the paradox is that if you are doing it well, it'll create a gap to move you out of that role. So it's easier for the powers that be to leave you where you are, and let inertia prevail. You must combat this. You don't get anything in this life without asking for it. So ask.

But asking is a skill – it needs to be done in the right way. You put your boss in an awkward place if you ask him for a promotion when it's hard for him to help you. So you need to seek out a particular task that's being neglected, and propose yourself as the one who can fix it, or wait until there are other changes going on – then press your case. You have to combine timing with opportunism.

When I was eighteen, and had failed to get into seven different universities, I fluked my way into a job as a lowly clerk in the number-crunching part of a large advertising agency. In my department there was a tedious task to be done, analysing dozens of market research reports. Because it was boring and time-consuming, nobody was racing to take it on. I ended up with it, so I worked day, night and weekend, for several weeks until I had produced an analysis I thought was really quite impressive. Then I showed it to the boss. I had saved more senior people a lot of trouble, and I had produced something good. I got no reward at the time, but I had shown myself as someone with the desire and the ability to be more than a clerk. In some dice games, you have to roll a six to start. I had rolled my six.

The fourth point is the most ironic. People most often get the promotion they crave by resigning. It's only when someone good is leaving that we fight to get them back, and that fight is usually manifested by offering the would-be leaver more money and a more senior job. In order for it to be worth your staying somewhere, you have to be willing to leave.

This is a card that needs to be played intelligently. You must accept the risk that your present boss may not fight to keep you as fiercely as you had hoped – so you have to go to the new job. Which means that you must never threaten to leave unless the new job is really worthwhile. In turn, that means that you must never be persuaded to stay in the old job, unless the improvements you're offered are really worthwhile. You should be given more responsibility, a title to reflect that, and more money too. Don't settle for less.

I said earlier that you shouldn't chase more money too directly, and I stand by that – except when you threaten to leave. If you say you're going, and they don't put more money on the table to make you stay, they don't want you badly enough. Take the new job.

Which brings me back neatly to my earlier point: only ever use the offer of a new job as a threat to improve your old job if you really want the new job. Your current employer may call your bluff, forcing you into the new job. So it has to be more than a bargaining chip; it has to be a real opportunity in its own right.

I'm not claiming that the path to promotion is easy: but at least it's clear.

Do your present job well; treat the people around you with warmth; and be brave enough to ask for what you want. If you ask for something you may not get it, but if you don't ask you certainly won't.

And if asking doesn't produce what you want, wait, and then ask again. Success in office life depends much less on brilliance and much more on persistence than you might think.

A car can be a brand, a bar of chocolate can be a brand. Can you be a brand?

What is a brand?

It's a product whose personality is so strong that it has disproportionate power in the market place. But that is to do with strength of character, not strength of sales. Porsche is a brand. Mercedes is a brand. But Ford or Toyota are not brands, even though they outsell Porsche or Mercedes by a mile. You might buy a Toyota because it's a good car, but you wouldn't buy it because it has Toyota written on the bonnet.

Yet being a brand isn't about exclusivity. After all, virtually every taxi in Europe seems to be a Mercedes, and there's nothing exclusive about getting a cab. Staying with cars, a Mini is a brand, even though it's small and inexpensive. Marlboro cigarettes are a brand, and so is a Mars Bar, and it's hardly exclusive to be available in every filling station or supermarket.

Yet all of these brands radiate a certain kind of confidence and charisma. It's hard to define, but it's easy to recognise.

People in business are preoccupied with the importance of brands, because we all instinctively defer to power, in whatever form it takes.

It's easy to forget that people can be brands too. In American politics Bill Clinton, in spite of his sexual peccadilloes and his unwillingness to tell the truth about them, is definitely a brand, whereas Jimmy Carter, a president of huge integrity, is not. In the world of business, Richard Branson and Terence Conran are brands, but Alan Sugar, in spite of a million television appearances, clearly is not.

What is it that sets people like Branson and Conran apart? The way they present themselves has much to do with it. Richard Branson always appears in jeans and an open-necked shirt, bearded, with a haircut which looks as if he's trying to impersonate an Afghan hound on a windy day. The metalanguage here (if you'll excuse a Media Studies term) is one of rebellion. He's saying 'I'm not a conventional business man. I'm one of the people. I'm young at heart. I do things differently.'

Terence Conran usually has his photograph taken when he is sprawled in a leather armchair, with a large Havana cigar on the go, and a generous glass of wine in his hand. The metalanguage here is one of the good life. He's saying, 'I'm relaxed. I know how to enjoy myself.'

Both these men brand themselves in a way which supports their business. The Conran reputation is embedded in the way we furnish our homes and the way we eat, so a personal brand which is all about living well is perfectly relevant. Branson's rebellious persona feeds directly to the image of Virgin Atlantic as the lively, young airline taking on the stodgy might of middle-aged British Airways.

Yet businessmen who become brands don't always rely on external signals, be they beard-and-jeans or cigar-and-wine-glass. Warren Buffet, the most celebrated of American investors and one of the world's richest men, dresses and presents himself as a rather downbeat, elderly businessman. But I suspect that his image of folksy ordinariness is carefully cultivated. Keeping his headquarters in sleepy Omaha, Nebraska, rather than sexy California or dynamic New York may be a genuine preference, but it is also a strong statement. It's saying that Buffet isn't fooled by glamorous appearances.

Talking about the way he dresses, he said, 'I buy expensive suits. They just look cheap on me.'

There's something about a man who, in spite of his huge wealth, is determinedly ordinary that makes people more likely to trust him with their money.

Being a brand does matter. Steve Jobs presented himself as the messiah of cutting-edge technology. That helped him build Apple into a colossal global business, and eroded the power of the mighty Microsoft led by the commercially brilliant but uncharismatic Bill Gates.

Do not, however, be trapped into thinking that these successes are all about appearance and presentation. Virgin genuinely does offer a livelier, fresher experience than British Airways. Conran's shops and restaurants brought something utterly new to London. Warren Buffet's investments have outperformed virtually all of his rivals. As for Apple, I'm typing this now on my MacBook with my iPhone on the table beside me.

These successes are rooted in substance not style. But the men who created them all understood the importance of style as a way of drawing attention to the substance, of making it salient. I've worked with Terence Conran closely over many years, and it's clear that he's a brilliant designer – but he's also a brilliant marketeer. He knows that it's no use having a great idea if you don't tell people about it. And one of the best ways of telling is to have a leader who is himself not just a spokesman for his vision, but a living symbol of it.

You may think, That's all very well for Terence Conran or Richard Branson, but what does it have to do with me?

The answer is simple: you can learn by studying success. And in this case, what you can learn is the power of making yourself a brand, of projecting a personality which radiates what you stand for. Don't think that you have to become a business leader before that's relevant. It's the other way round: if you project a vivid personality, you're more likely to end up as a business leader.

Does that mean you should start walking about clutching a large Havana cigar? Clearly not, but look behind the symbol to the underlying message. Conran's body language radiates a sense of living well. All of Steve Jobs's body language spoke of a mission to make technology innovative and exciting, and he was unvaryingly consistent with that theme. All of Branson's body language speaks of a rebellious freshness, and again he is utterly consistent in that. What you see in all these people is a clear vision of what they want to create, and that vision is embodied in how they behave – with unerring constancy.

At a more modest level you can define what your strengths are, and set about presenting yourself in a way which emphasises those strengths. Here's a simple example: while I was running a design business, I felt that a sense of business order and commercial ambition was what I could add to a creative business. So I made a point, in an environment where the dress code was 'anything goes', of being the one man in the office who always wore a suit. It helped me identify myself as the authority figure.

I used to work in a fashionable advertising agency with a man called Richard Hall. He didn't have the natural cool of many of his peers, but he was ambitious and intellectually bright. He decided to position himself as the brainy one. Whether that was a conscious decision or an instinctive one I never worked out. But the result was the same: he wore the most outrageously unkempt clothes, his hair looked not just untrimmed but untamed, and his always-broken spectacles were held in place with a repair fashioned from either Sellotape or Elastoplast. He looked like the Professor of Archaeology at a good redbrick university. Everybody loved him for it. In the somewhat pretentious world of advertising, he was the magnificently unpretentious one. He was successful, not just because he was clever, but because he branded himself as clever.

Some of the mannerisms I've described may seem trivial, but they all worked as outward signals of inner strengths. And that can be potent. So try to understand what it is that you offer which is distinctive; then find a simple way of radiating that.

Being a brand isn't just for Mars Bars and Mercedes: it can work for you too.

An American in Paris

The American in this case is not a person, but a company: Procter and Gamble, the giant US conglomerate. After the Second World War, P&G (like many big American corporations) embarked on a programme of ambitious international expansion. One of the countries where they wanted to build a business was France. They had already bought a business in Britain – Thomas Hedley & Co. – so they had a bridgehead to Europe. France was to be the next step, and their first incursion into mainland Europe.

But France was different: in England, they had bought an existing business to build on, but in France they had nothing.

Nothing, that is, except an ambition – which, as we will see, can take you a long way.

Their first step was to promote one of their own rising stars to lead the new business. Unusually – for a US corporation pinning all their hopes on one man – he was not an American, but a bright and original Englishman, whom P&G had acquired when they bought

Thomas Hedley. His name was Tom Bower, and he had a gift for solving problems in an imaginative but ruthless way.

Tom took on the task of opening P&G in France in the mid-1950s. In England we had only just got used to the end of rationing for petrol and sweets (yes, really) but in America expansion was everything. Cars were growing fins longer and larger by the day, and chrome suppliers were struggling to keep pace. The word 'globalisation' may not have been invented yet, but the idea certainly had been.

But it was also a time when American desire to take over new territories commercially was not matched by much sensitivity to the people who happened to be living there. 'Yanks Go Home' was daubed unceremoniously across many a European wall. Tom Bower was shrewd enough to see this, and to realise what a problem it could be.

So he worked out a plan; he made his list; and he got on the phone.

His plan was simple: he would start by identifying the jobs he needed done by his key team. He wanted someone who knew about production, someone who knew about marketing, a legal expert, a finance expert, and so on. He listed about half a dozen crucial responsibilities, and set about recruiting the right people to fill those roles.

So far, so commonsensical. Now comes the good bit. Each of these people had to meet two criteria – they had to understand P&G culture (which in practice meant they had to be already on the P&G payroll) and *they had to speak fluent French*.

Tom went painstakingly through all the P&G human resources files and found someone in P&G with relevant experience for each role, with a good track record, *and with the ability to speak French like a Frenchman.*

Then Tom rang each of them. Making the calls must have taken a bit of stage management – bear in mind that Tom had never met any of these people, and many of them lived and worked far away. The marketing guy, for example, was working for P&G in South East Asia. Tom rang him on a Thursday morning, Asian time. He introduced himself, explained that he was in charge of setting up the new P&G operation in France, said what an exciting opportunity this was, and then announced that the man in question was to be the first Marketing Director of P&G France. He went on to say that the man was booked on a flight to Paris that Saturday (his wife and young children could come later, Tom kindly explained) and a room was reserved for him in the Georges V.

'I've never been there,' Tom said, 'but I'm told it's a nice hotel.' (It certainly is a 'nice' hotel: one of the best in Paris and arguably one of the best in the world.)

Tom went on to explain that the rest of the team would also be flying into Paris that Saturday, and were all staying in the Georges V, until they'd had the time to find something more permanent.

The newly appointed marketing guy, still very stunned, said he was looking forward to meeting his new boss, Tom, there.

'Oh no,' said Tom, 'It's a crucial policy of mine that this thing can only succeed if all the top management team can speak good French. I don't speak a word, so I'm going on an immersion course in French, and I won't join you till I'm fluent.'

'Don't worry,' he added, 'the manager of the Georges V already has a banker's draft for one million dollars which he can give you when you arrive. That should give you something to get offices with, and then you can get on with starting the business.'

At this point Tom wished his new Marketing Director the best of luck, and put the phone down.

And that is how one of the world's largest companies launched its business in France. The team (minus Tom, of course) did all meet in the Georges V on the Saturday, got to know each other, and laid plans for the new company. Tom, who unsurprisingly turned out to be a quick learner and a natural linguist, joined them two months later, speaking French convincingly. The business in France became a success. P&G expanded into Germany, then Italy, and was soon on its way to being the global force it is today.

This is, I believe, a brilliant example of leadership in action. Of course, by today's standards, the uprooting of half a dozen people and their families from one country to another with no room for discussion and only hours of notice seems ruthless to the point of brutality. (Although being forced to have a highly paid job in Paris is a hardship most of us could come to terms with.)

But by every other criterion, it was a brilliantly planned and brilliantly executed stratagem. What can we learn from it?

First, Tom understood the importance of a good team of people as the basis of any business. Good business ultimately always hinges on good people.

Second, his insistence that anyone working in France must speak good French showed a vivid understanding of the importance of going into local markets on their terms, not yours.

The idea that 'we do it that way at home so we can do it that way abroad' is precisely why so many good companies fail when they try to expand internationally.

And the shock value in the French business community of an American company opening in Paris *with an entirely French-speaking management* must have been electrifyingly positive.

Third, Tom's plan was carefully worked out and researched before being put into practice – but the pace with which it was then executed was both breathtaking and bold. It gave no time for debate and doubt, and it laid a foundation stone for the culture of the business in the future: deeds count more than words.

Don't imagine that the French-speaking thing is only relevant to international businesses. It's symptomatic of realising that your customers – wherever they are – are more important than you are. *You need to speak their language; whether that's literally or figuratively.*

There's an amusing postscript to this tale. On that first weekend when the new team met on a Saturday morning – strangers suddenly thrust into a new job in a new place – they were at first quite grateful to be comforted by the luxurious surroundings of the Georges V. But by Sunday night they'd had enough of chandeliers and champagne, and wanted to go out and enjoy a beer and a hamburger. But they had no French money, and while there was a one million dollar banker's draft in the hotel safe, the hotel manager had gone home (it was Sunday night after all) and no one else knew the combination. So they tried to explain to the barman that they wanted to borrow enough cash for half a dozen beers and burgers; and their credit was good for a million US dollars in the morning.

You can imagine how believable that was.

The car of your dreams: a modern parable

T here's a book you should read. (Apart from this one, of course.)

It's written by an American named Martin Mayer and the book is called *Madison Avenue, USA*. It was written in the late 1950s, a time when the American economy was growing explosively. After victory in the Second World War, the USA was establishing itself as the one unchallengeable world superpower.

The theme of Mayer's book is the importance of advertising as a crucial driver of that unprecedented economic expansion. Remember that this was written at a time when modern advertising techniques were first being invented: it was the dawn of marketing as we now understand it. Mayer argues that the ability of sophisticated marketing techniques to stimulate demand lay at the heart of America's burgeoning prosperity.

Mayer opines that it was not just modern advertising, but the market research that underpinned it, that was generating this great miracle of surging consumer demand. Advertising for big companies would *inevitably* be effective, Mayer states, because big companies had the resources and the knowledge to call on market research techniques so foolproof that the success of their new ventures could be guaranteed.

He doesn't just make this claim in general terms; he gives a specific real-life example to prove his point. He cites the extravagant launch of a new car by one of America's automobile giants – a car that had been so thoroughly market researched, using the best and latest research techniques, that its future success was utterly certain. It simply could not fail. Mayer wrote this case history just before the new car was launched, so confident was he.

But life doesn't always turn out quite like we expect. Not just for you and me, but for Martin Mayer too. Because the case history of inevitable success which Mayer chose was the launch of the Ford Edsel – which turned out to be far and away the largest catastrophe in the history of the car industry. Anywhere. Ever.

Ford lost $2.5 billion on the disaster that was Edsel.

The Edsel was intended to be the car of all our dreams. And Ford's research *proved* that it was. Every inch of the Edsel – the car, the name, the advertising, the everything – were all researched to within an inch of their lives. Except that in real life (as opposed to life on Planet Research) the Edsel sank like a stone. The car of our dreams became the car of Ford's nightmares.

Which demonstrates that market research is a lot less reliable than market research companies would have us believe.

What went wrong? Bearing in mind that it doesn't get much 'wronger' than a loss of $2.5 billion.

The answer is depressingly simple. Market research tells us vividly what people like – in terms of what they are familiar with now. But it can't tell us how people will react to a *new* idea. It purports to do this, but the truth is that most of us are good at understanding how we feel and behave now, but bad at imagining how things could be done differently.

Of course, market research tries to explore how people will react to new ideas, but it does it spectacularly badly, for two very good reasons.

First, the kind of folk who are drawn to work in market research are analytical types, not creative thinkers. They are classically perfect examples of left-brain thinkers. But to have a good sense of *how things might be* rather than *how things are* needs a right-brain mindset – an ability to think laterally, even illogically. Market researchers aren't like that: they get the numerical and analytical stuff, but they're usually tone deaf to creative and lateral values.

I have met some wonderful exceptions to this rule, but believe me, like friendly parking wardens, they are a treasured minority.

Second, most of us just aren't astute at anticipating how we'd react in new circumstances. If an idea is outside the comfort zone of our present knowledge and experience, it's human nature to be sceptical. Someone who understood this better than most was Henry Ford – the founder of Ford Motor Company, and the man who democratised the motor car.

When asked why he didn't research his ideas with the public, he replied, 'If I had asked people what they wanted, they'd have said faster horses.'

What a cruel irony that it was the same Ford family, generations later, who burned up $2.5 billion of shareholder's money with the disastrous launch of the over-researched but under-imagined Ford Edsel.

Why did the Edsel fail? It was the equivalent in its time of a 'faster horse' in the sense that it took current tastes to the ultimate. American cars had been getting increasingly bigger, clumsier, more bejewelled with chrome. The Edsel was the paradigm of that ideal. Of course it looked in market research like a certain winner. It embodied the best of what the public was used to.

The **EDSEL LOOK** is here to stay
—and 1959 cars will prove it!

Less than fifty dollars difference between Edsel and V-8's in the Low-Priced Three

But sometimes the public has an unconscious yearning for something quite different, even though they often don't recognise that consciously. It's only when a different product comes along, which chimes with that yearning, that the public realises what it is that they've been wanting.

Soon after the catastrophe that was Edsel, the Volkswagen Beetle started to become a cult car in the US. It was everything the Edsel wasn't. It was also everything the American public wouldn't have wanted in a market research survey. Indeed a famous advertisement for the Beetle in America at the time used the provocative headline 'Think Small'. At a time in America when bigger was assumed to be better, promoting smallness as a virtue was revolutionary. But this brave advertisement anticipated a shift in the zeitgeist. Suddenly, to be functional was more esteemed than to be flamboyant. Opulance had been a virtue: now it was a limitation.

The world had changed. It wasn't just the USA. In Britain, the Mini was launched. There had not been a small car like it before: it was designed as a small car, not a big car reduced. It was tiny outside, yet roomy inside, it was practical, it was different, it was fun.

Thanks to its unconventional design, the Mini was slow to catch on. But as it became more familiar, people started to love it and it became a runaway success. Half a century later, the design of today's small cars still owes much to the thinking that created the Mini.

Both the Mini and the Beetle were the masterpieces of genuinely original designers, who relied on their own vision, not someone else's market research.

The relevance of this to office life today is massive. In a tough world economy, every business wants to be sure before it spends. Whether it's a new product, a new package, or a new TV commercial, big corporations want evidence that their project is going to work before they press the start button.

But as we've seen, that evidence is often an illusion. And the more innovative an idea is, the more likely it is that research will give the wrong answer.

This begs a rather large question: if research isn't the answer, what is?

To unlock this, a good discipline is to think of some of the great works of art you admire. In architecture, are you moved by the strange shapes of the Guggenheim museum in Bilbao? Or the massive dignity of St Paul's cathedral? Or both? In painting, do you admire the febrile imagination of Salvador Dali, the extraordinary vision of Goya, or the gracious compositions of Manet? You must make your own list, but choose a handful of works – buildings, paintings, novels, poetry, whatever – that truly stir you. Now consider what it was that made those great works possible, beyond the genius of the people who produced them.

The answer is simple: on top of their great talent, the creators of these great works were *willing to take a risk*.

A very big risk, as it often turned out.

Sir Christopher Wren was vilified when St Paul's cathedral was built; his design just didn't conform to the expectations of others. When Goya painted *The Clothed Maja* and *The Naked Maja*, perhaps two of the most significant paintings of that century, the Spanish Inquisition expelled him from his job as official painter to the Spanish royal court. Manet's greatest masterpiece, *Déjeuner sur l'herbe* was brutally rejected from the salon for which it was painted. Manet had to create the Salon des Refusés a kind of rejects club, to get his picture shown to the public.

Works of art which endure into the future often seem dangerously uncomfortable in the present – as Wren, Goya and Manet discovered. But these great men were willing to risk the opprobrium of today to create something that would be admired tomorrow. They were wise enough to know that new ideas can seem shocking at first, and they were brave enough to take that risk.

Humbler though the office world is, exactly the same principles apply. Don't expect new ideas to be easy at the beginning. But recognise that they are really the only ideas worth having in the long run. Without research to tell you what's good and bad, you have to rely on your own judgement (which isn't so frightening really: isn't your judgement what you're getting paid to use?).

Every new idea that we now accept as a useful part of our normal life needed someone to take a risk to get that idea to happen in the first place. Imagine that the bicycle had never been invented, and someone described the idea of a bike to you: you'd think that this two-wheeled gravity-defying thing couldn't possibly stay safely upright for more than two seconds. But somehow, the bike got invented, got accepted, and is now one of the world's most popular forms of transport.

Similarly, there was a time when, if you wanted to get cash from your bank account, you went to your local branch (only open until 3.00 p.m., closed all weekend) waited in a long queue, and eventually presented your cheque. It was a ludicrously slow and cumbrous way of people getting to their own money. But you can bet when the idea of a hole-in-the-wall cash machine was first mooted, there'd have been howls of protest: where would you install these things, how would you keep the money safe, how would you stop theft by the machine, and so on. Now we can't imagine life without the cash machine.

And social historians will tell you that the bikini – that essential in any young woman's holiday packing – caused widespread moral outrage when it first appeared.

It's painfully clear that people's instinct is to distrust new ideas: until they get used to them, and then we conveniently forget that we ever had doubts.

Which is why research will never help you with a genuinely new concept. To get new things to happen, *you* have to take a risk. That will call for courage, and persuasiveness too, as you will have to take other people with you. But without risk you will achieve nothing remarkable.

And as the costly tale of the Ford Edsel demonstrates, the best market research doesn't take the risk away – it just hides it from you until it's too late.

Does that mean I should never use market research?

In spite of everything I've said in the last chapter, market research can be hugely useful. But you have to know how and when.

The last chapter was concerned with the inadequacy of research as a way of learning how people will respond to new ideas. But while research doesn't work for tomorrow's thinking, it's great at defining what is happening today. I gave the example of a cash machine as something people would find hard to grasp if they'd never seen one. But if you had researched the behaviour and attitudes of people in the days before cash machines, you would have found two things.

First, they could only go to the bank to get cash in their lunch hour, because they were at work the rest of the time. Second, that meant that they had to endure tiresomely long queues to get their money, as everyone else was trying to get cash at the same time as they were.

This research would have made it clear that the existing method of obtaining cash was not working well for the customer, so there was a real opportunity for a new system. The research would have defined the problem clearly. It just wouldn't have defined the answer – that kind of creative thinking is your job.

Knowing what your customers are doing and thinking today is essential for any business. Market research can help massively in that.

The key is to distinguish between research that is looking at what people do and think now – very useful – and research that predicts how they will react tomorrow – deeply dangerous.

As a postscript, don't overlook the hard truth that the best research of all is your own sales figures. They show exactly how people value your product. There is no better test of someone's belief in a product than their willingness to part with their money in order to experience it.

When the latest sales figures arrive in a company, there is a great tendency – if they are disappointing – to find some explanation. The sales look bad because we are comparing them with an unusually good period last year; the sales look bad because everyone went away for Easter. Believe me, I've heard more excuses than you can imagine. But excuses are all they are: if the sales look bad, it's usually because the sales are bad. Don't allow yourself, or your colleagues, to be in denial. You have a problem. It's best to own up to that, and deal with it.

The power of 'No'

'**N**o' may be one of the shortest words in the English language, but it's still one of the hardest to say. We all hate to be rejected, so we instinctively avoid inflicting rejection on others. And saying 'no' is always a kind of rejection.

Yet to be successful, we have to come to grips with 'No'. It may be a difficult word, but it's also a powerful word, and sometimes a very necessary word.

Here are some examples:

Someone asks you for a raise, when money is tight and it can't be justified.

You get asked to take on a project which seems a step backwards for you, not a step forwards.

You get asked to give someone special treatment, which others don't enjoy.

You get shown a proposal which simply isn't good enough.

I could go on: the list is endless.

The natural tendency is to try to be helpful; you want to accommodate the other person as much as you can. But ironically, being 'helpful' can end up causing more problems than it solves. You give someone a raise they don't really deserve – result, word gets out (it always does) and suddenly ten other people are asking for raises. You take on a project that's not pushing your career forward – result, you get taken advantage of again and again.

I felt the problem keenly when I worked in advertising. It's a trade where you're endlessly being asked to approve creative ideas by the people who produced them. Saying their idea isn't good enough is like telling a mother that her baby is ugly. Instant tantrum, and you seem to have made an enemy for life.

So, even though you know the idea is not right, you try to deal with it kindly. You say it's *nearly* right, when your heart tells you it's plain wrong. You even start to kid yourself that the idea is almost good enough, because subconsciously you don't want to hurt someone else's feelings. Besides, you don't want to portray yourself as the office brute.

This softer approach makes a bad situation worse. If you tell someone their idea is nearly right, they'll believe you. So they'll tweak the idea a bit to allow for your concerns. You'll see it again, in modified form, but if it's still fundamentally the same idea, it's still fundamentally wrong. Trouble is, you can't say that now, because at the last meeting you said it was nearly right. If you had said a firm 'no' at the outset, you might have made people cross at the time, but at least you've been clear and honest. And if a creative idea is wrong, it's always better to tear it up and have a fresh start, than try to modify something that's never really going to be good enough.

Similarly, if someone makes an unreasonable request, it's tempting to give them some of what they ask for, to keep the peace. For instance, they ask for a 10 per cent bonus, when 5 per cent is the rule; you end up giving them 7 per cent. They don't thank you for it, as it wasn't what they wanted, and when others discover it, they'll accuse you of unfairness and favouritism. And they'll be right.

If you're early in your career, you may think this doesn't apply to you – you're not at the stage when you are being asked for raises and bonuses.

Don't you believe it: at every level in office life you'll be confronted with the need to express an opinion. And how you respond determines how others think about you.

But herein lies the irony: you believe, by being gentle, that you will be liked. Tragically incorrect: you won't be seen as being gentle, you'll be seen as being weak. At any rate, smart people don't go to work wanting to be liked – they want to be respected. Respect leads to promotion and to power: affection just leads to someone to have a drink with when you get passed over for promotion.

Of all the gifts which make a good leader, clarity and decisiveness are two of the most potent. 'No' may not be the word someone wants to hear. But if it's the word that needs to be said, at least it's clear, and everyone knows where they stand. And when you say 'No' it shows you as strong and decisive.

It's surprising how many problems at work begin because someone would rather be liked than respected, and so they don't have the courage to say 'No' when they should.

If you can find that courage, and learn to use 'No' when you need to, you're on the way to being a leader.

You can't achieve success if you can't describe it

In athletics, if a runner crosses the line first, he's the winner. It doesn't matter whether the runner behind him was a tenth of a second away or came in twenty minutes later – the winner is still the winner. In a football match, if the ball goes in the net, then it's a goal: and if it doesn't, then it isn't. The supporting crowd leaps to their feet if a goal is scored; and there is a huge collective groan if it is missed. Part of the excitement of sport is the clarity of success. Everyone – players and spectators alike – know what success means.

In office life, people are often much less clear about where the goalposts are, about where the target is. Is the aim of a project to drive costs down or to drive sales up? If it's a campaign to drive sales up, by how much do we need to do that in order to recoup the cost of the campaign?

Too many projects fail just because the journey doesn't start with a clear definition of what the destination is.

It's a bizarre truth that most people in most companies only have a crude idea of what the company's profit is. Yet that profit is what determines success for the shareholders, and it's what means job security and salary rises for the staff.

Companies often have a strange reluctance to discuss profits with their staff: it's as if talking about profit is taboo, because if it has to be improved, that means it's too low now, and if it's too low now, then that's a sign of weakness. But if you don't face weakness you'll never conquer it. How can we expect people to grow the profit if they don't know what it is in the first place?

At any rate, in my experience the staff in a business usually have a shrewd sense of how well or badly the business is doing, regardless of whether their bosses confide in them or not. So the bosses who do confide earn respect from the staff because they treat their staff like grown-ups.

Put simply, you're much more likely to score if you know exactly where the goalposts are. If you are briefing a project to a team, it's crucial to be clear and simple about what you want them to do. And it's important to put a definite number on it. If it's a push to improve sales, it's not enough to say you want more sales, you need to be specific about exactly what percentage sales increase you are all aiming at. If you are in the team being briefed, and you don't get this information, then ask for it. A good boss will see the value of your question. A bad boss may resent it, and may even take that out on you, but if you're working for a duffer you're going to have to deal with that sooner or later anyway.

When success is being defined it's vital to be clear and candid about what is needed, and to quantify the target. But it's also vital to keep it simple. Stick to one unvarnished objective. If someone unexpectedly throws you a tennis ball, you'll catch it, instinctively. If they throw you four, you'll drop them all. It's the same with ideas. Give a person one clear idea, and they'll grasp it. Give them several, and instantly confusion takes over. The objective of a project at work is no different: if the ambition is utterly simple, people can get it, and they can respond to it. Complicate it and you've lost them.

When the brilliant Gerry Robinson started his career as an entrepreneur, he bought a little-known catering company called Compass from a large conglomerate. He then floated the company on the stock exchange, and set about building it into a much more profitable business. He owned some of the shares, so his personal wealth depended on growing the company – if the share price grew, the value of his personal stake would grow. So the share price was crucial to him, and his partners. Gerry decided that if everyone focused on that, it was more likely to happen. He therefore installed a large notice board bang in the middle of the company's reception, with the current share price displayed on it. It was updated hourly.

It was an odd thing to do. I've never seen it done in any other business. Companies' share prices are publicly available – you can easily find them on the web or in the papers. But because things look bad if a company's share price falls, flaunting your share price in your head office reception seems a risk. You'd be a hostage to fortune if the price started to fall. But it was a risk Gerry was happy to take if it enabled him to define crisply what success looked like for the business. It was a magnificently simple way of telling the staff, and everyone who visited the offices, that this was a company that cared about its share price, and was determined to grow that share price. Everyone knew where the goalposts were.

That was several years ago. Now Gerry is happily retired in his Donegal mansion with a massive fortune. Compass is the largest catering company in the world: its value on the stock market is an astonishing £13 billion. That's not a misprint: I really mean billion, not million.

Of course that extraordinary growth depended on many different people and many different ideas. But in the formative years, it was Gerry's single-minded sense of purpose which drove the business, reinforced by his passion to make vivid to everyone just what success looked like.

So it's vital to have a sharply defined vision of what the aim is, of what constitutes success. But that vision means nothing unless it's communicated to the team who have to deliver it. The ambition must be simple and clear, but it must also be understood and shared by everyone involved in making it a reality.

Once that ambition has been communicated, the next stage is to measure regularly how things are going. If we need to increase turnover by 10 per cent in a year, what increase do we have after three months? If we're a quarter of the way through the year, we should be a quarter of the way to our target.

For a few years I was Chairman of a big PR company. It had great turnover, but lousy profits. My aim was to put that right, to get the profits up to something significant. I booked a big conference hall near the head office, and made everyone (really everyone, including the receptionist and the cook) come to a meeting after work. I took them through the performance of the business, showing them the actual figure for the high turnover and the actual figure for the low profit. I spelt out that the definition of success was to boost the profit figure. Every other objective, however worthy, was subsidiary to that. Some of the staff were a bit shocked to see the poor profit. For others, it confirmed their suspicions. But for all of them, the target was now clear.

So I had communicated the ambition. The next step was to measure how well we were achieving it. I set up a bonus scheme where the top forty people in the company got a predetermined share of any profit we made over our target. Then every month, we got those forty people in a room, and we updated them on what was happening in the business, good and bad. Crucially, we showed them the latest profit results, and how big (or how small) their bonus pool was.

They knew the target, they knew whether we were hitting it, and they knew how that affected them personally. Over a three year period, we increased the profit seven-fold. I know that it's much easier to improve on a small number than a big one, but a seven times increase on a small base is still not bad. Of course we were doing lots of other stuff to make the business better, but I'm convinced that much of our success came from having a clear aim, watching to see whether we were delivering it, and rewarding the staff well if we did.

I started this chapter with the concept that in order to inspire people to achieve success you must first describe to them what success look like. The target must be clear. But when you have created success, you must then celebrate it. Motivating people doesn't stop when the job stops – otherwise they won't be motivated for you when the next job comes along.

What do I mean by celebrating success? Do we all go out to a wine bar and get drunk? Well, that may be a part of it, but it's the least important part. The first thing to do is to get everyone together and tell them exactly what has been achieved. Give specific results and show how they compare with the original plan. Then thank everyone. Give the most generous thanks to the people who had the least glamorous roles. They'll appreciate being appreciated, and the more senior people will see that you're being gracious.

Thanking matters more than you might think. There's an astute American businessman called Robert Townend, who had great success at Avis, the car hire company, and then wrote a very witty book about his experiences. In his book, he refers eloquently to 'thanks' as a 'much-neglected form of compensation'. It's a thought to reflect on. How often in office life do we stand up and say 'thank you'? It's a powerful phrase, especially when it's stated in public.

Giving thanks is a currency which costs nothing to the giver but has huge value to the receiver.

Once you have thanked them, let the team swap their war stories, give them a beer or a glass of wine, and let them get on with it. But the hospitality shouldn't be flamboyant: celebrating success is about getting everyone together somewhere they feel comfortable, not somewhere they feel intimidated.

There is one last tricky point: what happens if you don't have a success to celebrate? The answer, surprisingly perhaps, is that you celebrate failure. Get everyone together and tell them what has been achieved; show the good bits and show the bad bits; and thank everyone for their efforts even though they didn't get the result you wanted. After that you can discuss what you've all learnt, and how you could do it better the next time. You can hold back on the champagne; you're not pretending this was a success. You're acknowledging that it was a failure, but you're still a team and you want to improve.

If you deal with failures with that sense of honesty and that respect for teamwork, maybe the next celebration will be a success.

Do I dare to start my own business?

These could be eight of the most significant words you ever ask yourself. It's something that, if you're ambitious, you're almost certain to ponder at some stage in your career. If you do make the big leap, you are in for more stress and risk – and more possibilities – than you could imagine. But if you stand endlessly on the brink, yet never make that leap, you will never know what might have been.

If you do get tempted to start up on your own, you will quickly find that you have an unending list of tasks: finding a good accountant, getting offices, creating your own website, raising the money, and so on. But I firmly believe that, important though all these things are, there are just two things which matter more than all of the others added together. These two things are *passion* and a *strong central idea*.

Passion is crucial. Get this wrong and you could lose your self-belief and your life savings. Get it right, and you could be fulfilled beyond your dreams. You won't be able to navigate a journey that testing without a massive reservoir of passion to draw on. Put simply, *you have to want this with a deep emotional hunger if you are going to win.*

What do I mean by a strong central idea?

If you're going to start a new business you must have a confident, but simple, concept of what that business offers that makes it special.

Think about all the different people you'll need to sell your business idea to. Obviously, you have to win over customers. But you have to convince staff to join you too; persuade the bank to lend you the money you need; get suppliers to give you credit; and the landlord of your first office to sign a lease with you. All of these people need to believe in your idea. So it's crucial that you can describe that idea in just one compelling sentence.

There's an American concept called the 'elevator pitch'. The notion is that you get in a lift with someone who could be influential, and you have a few seconds to sell them your idea in the time it takes to get from the fifth floor to the ground. It may sound glib, but it's a brutally good test: if you don't have a strong elevator pitch, you probably won't have a strong business either.

A strong central idea isn't something which just happens, like rainfall or sunshine. You have to work on it. If you want to start a cafe, for instance, how will it be different from other cafes, and how will you make that difference real?

When I worked in advertising, I wanted for many years to start my own agency. I was searching endlessly for a point of difference.

Eventually, it struck me that advertising agencies always seemed to lose money on small clients, and make money on large ones. Yet they ceaselessly chase after clients of any size. Why not just create an advertising agency which only handled large projects? And to make that credible, why not restrict the number of clients we'd work with to twelve? While our rivals greedily went after everything and anything, we'd be selective about who we worked with. We'd concentrate on the quality of our clients, not the quantity.

Of course, other advertising agencies scoffed at this, but it gave us a point of difference, a story to tell. And we did end up working with a relatively short list of big companies, so we did deliver the promise in practice.

Another, particularly vivid example of the strong central idea also comes from the world of advertising. When Nigel Bogle, John Bartle and John Hegarty set up their own advertising agency in the 1980s, they decided that their big idea was to produce advertising which was highly distinctive. Nothing very original in that, you might think – what advertising agency isn't aiming to do distinctive work? But what made Bartle Bogle Hegarty's position stand out was the way they promoted their idea. They used the simple but memorable line 'When the world zigs, zag' to define themselves; they used a black sheep as a symbol of their vision; and they even had a black sheep in their reception. Above all, they produced ads for people like Levi's, Audi and Lynx which lived up to their claim. Their agency is now a world-wide business, admired and successful; their creative head, John Hegarty, is now Sir John, and if you can't find him in his office he may well be in his beautiful vineyard in the South of France.

I can't stress too strongly how vital it is to begin with a clear central idea, and an overdose of passion.

Let's assume you've got those two main ingredients – now what?

At this point you have to balance two conflicting forces. On the one hand, you need to plan every aspect of the new business. What's it going to be called? Who are you going to do it with? Where will you work from? How much money do you need? This has to cover everything, from the big points right down to the detail of designing your business card and finding a good accountant.

But on the other hand, you also have to do it. You must have a well thought-out plan. It's vital to look before you leap. But the point comes when you have to make that leap. And that's when careful planning needs to be balanced by raw courage.

This dilemma between thorough planning and willingness to act is a classic example of the tension between left-brain thinking – 'I must plan it properly before I do anything' – and right-brain thinking – 'I want to do it, so I'll do it.'

I'm perhaps a bad person to give advice on this. My own nature can be impulsive and impatient, so I'm inclined to leap without doing enough looking first. Clearly, you need to get the balance right. But I'd argue that, since it's rarely possible to pitch the balance absolutely perfectly, if you're going to get it slightly wrong, it's better to be a bit hasty than to overplan. If you're too hasty you can correct mistakes as you go, but if you're overly thoughtful there's a real danger that you'll never get off the ground. If it's in you to start your own business, you'll never forgive yourself if you dream the dream but fail to make it a reality.

Your own business: making the dream a reality

In the last chapter I made much of the need – if you want to be your own boss – to have a good dose of passion and a strong central idea for the business. If you now feel you have plucked up the courage to strike out on your own, that you have that commitment and that core idea, what happens next?

This is where you need to change gear from right brain to left brain. You have the passion, now you need the plan.

However fired up you may be, you now need to translate ambition into organisation. Plan your project like a military campaign. Sit yourself down somewhere quiet, with proper time and a blank pad. Now make a list of every detail which needs to be resolved. Don't deal with them at this stage, just list them. The idea is not to solve problems, but to identify them – to create a checklist of all the tasks you'll need to work through to create your battle plan.

Here are some of the things I suggest need to be on your list:

Finance: How much money will you need? How much of this can you afford to put in? Where will the rest come from? If some of the money is borrowed, will you be able to pay it back?

Income: How much will you expect to earn from your customers, and how long will it take for that money to come in?

Stock: Do you have to buy stuff before you sell it, and if so, how much do you need, and who will supply you?

Offices: Can you work from home, and if so, will that look small-time to others? If you need an office, where, and at what cost?

Equipment: What kit do you need? Almost certainly a laptop and some software, but what else?

Partners: Are you doing this on your own? It's a tough journey if you do. But equally, if you're you doing it with partners, it's crucial to make the right choice: you're going to be together for a long time.

Who owns the business? When you start up, you should own 100 per cent. But it's easy to see that whittled away, as you give shares to partners or to people who are putting money in. You have to incentivise others, but once you've started to share out that 100 per cent you'll never get it back. It's better to be selfish at the beginning, if you can get away with it.

Bank: You'll need a friendly bank manager. Even if he's not putting money in, he's still potentially an important ally.

Accountant: The same applies. Talk to friends who've done something similar, and use their advice and their contacts. Having a good accountant will help you stay sane.

Lawyer: Do you need one? Yes, you do. You have to decide whether it's going to be set up as a limited company, a limited liability partnership, or something different. That may sound a bit technical, but it matters. If it all goes horribly wrong, limited liability means you may lose a lot, but you shouldn't lose everything. Again, get advice from people you know, and don't settle on a lawyer until you feel comfortable with who you have found. In day-by-day business, you won't see your bank manager, your accountant or your lawyer often – but when you do, it'll be important. It's worth getting these relationships right.

Staff: Who else do you need to get things going? Too many people means that the business will struggle under the weight of too much cost, but too few may stop you getting the work done. In my experience, it's usually best to start with as few people as possible, but to make sure they're good.

The prize: What do you want to get out of it? This may sound obvious, but people starting up on their own are usually so driven by pride, and the desire to get going, that they fail to think through all the longer-term financial implications. For instance, people starting up on their own usually pay themselves much less than they'd get on the open market. That's wise: you need to think frugal in business, especially at the outset. But it's easy to forget, after a few years on a low salary, that at some point you'd like to get back the earnings you've sacrificed. Work out what your real future ambitions are, financially and in other ways.

The pitch: What is the big promise that will get this business airborne, and how are you going to publicise it?

I'm sure there's more, but that's quite enough to give you a flavour. List all of the things you're going to have to deal with, and when you have your list, work through it, item by item, spelling out your plan under each point.

Then you need to piece together these bits of the jigsaw into one coherent business plan, which shows how much you expect to get as turnover, what your costs will be, and how much profit can be made. Some of this is going to be guesswork: obviously, you can't tell how many customers a business will have until it's started trading. But there's a big difference between guesswork and intelligent guesswork. Do all that you can to make your plans and forecasts as realistic as possible. It always takes longer than you think for income to come in, and people pay you more slowly than you'd like. The cost to you of getting work done is usually more than you expect. I don't mean that in a gloomy way – an entrepreneur has to be an optimist. But an entrepreneur has to be a wise and realistic optimist, not a naive one.

When I started in business, I asked someone I respected greatly how he judged the plan for a new business venture.

'Simple,' he replied. 'If the business plan shows the original investment gets paid back in less than three years, I dismiss it as unrealistically optimistic. But if the business plan shows the original investment gets paid back in more than three years, I dismiss it because it's not profitable enough.'

In a way he was teasing me, yet in a way he wasn't. What he was looking for was a plan which made money in a decent time period: if it doesn't do that in theory it certainly won't in practice, and if it won't in practice, why bother? But he was also looking for a plan which he trusted – anything that seemed too quick and too easy on paper wouldn't deliver in real life.

This takes us back to the tension between right-brain and left-brain thinking. The right brain will tell you to go ahead and do it, because it's passionate and ambitious. The left brain will caution you to think through whether you can really make it work.

There is no clear answer to this conundrum. You will have to look at your plan and make your judgement. All I will say is that most entrepreneurs tend to be right-brain weighted; and most employees tend to be left-brain weighted. Do you want to end your career as an employee or an employer?

The crucial role of skirt length in business strategy: a true story from France (where else?)

An extraordinary event occurred in France in 1968. It was a time of huge social unrest across the nation. Students started to riot, in a dramatic and often violent way. Suddenly the workers of France caught the bug and before you could say '*mon dieu*' there was a general strike across the country. France ground to a halt.

This true tale concerns two of the world's largest manufacturing powers, and how they responded to the strike. The two companies were Procter and Gamble, usually known as P&G, and their great rivals Unilever. Both made the basic household products like soap and detergent that we use every day: indeed between them they dominated the market (as they still do) for this kind of product across the globe – including, of course, France. They both faced the massive crisis in France of seeing everything stop overnight: no factories working, so no production, so no sales, so no money, so . . .

What could they possibly do?

At the time, the head of P&G in France was a charismatic and maverick Englishman called Tom Bower. We've met Tom in an earlier chapter and, as we've seen, Tom was clever. But there are different ways of being clever, and Tom's cleverness was not a philosophical/intellectual kind of cleverness, it was a much more pragmatic kind of cleverness. Tom was not so much interested in ideas, he was interested in *ideas that worked.*

Tom sat down and had a good think about the problem he and his business faced. He knew his enemies at Unilever would be doing this too. Given what he knew of their management style, he imagined that they would be looking at the problem intellectually. Obviously they couldn't stop a national strike, so they would probably be setting up committees to model the economic impact of the strike, to look at how the financial effect of the strike would vary according to the length of the strike, and so forth.

Tom decided to look at things rather differently. He had no appetite for academic analysis: he wanted an action plan. And, imaginative man that he was, he came up with one.

A day or two later, Tom phoned one of the secretaries from his office. She, like everyone else, was at home because the factory and the adjoining office had been closed by the strike. Since she wasn't working, Tom asked, would she like to meet him for lunch that day?

So they had lunch and Tom explained his plan.

He had chosen the secretary carefully: she was a lively, enthusiastic woman, and loyal to the company. She had two small children, so the threat of the strike running on for weeks was greater for her than some of the other secretaries who didn't have children. And she was very pretty. (Before you imagine that this story exploits women, please hear me out: I think you'll find it's men that are exploited.)

She listened to Tom's plan, and she agreed.

What Tom wanted was the artwork for the packaging of their largest-selling brand of detergent. This artwork was in the office, which was surrounded by strike pickets. No one could penetrate the barrier of pickets. Well, almost no one.

The secretary arrived at the picket line the next morning. She was wearing a very short skirt, and a shy smile. Otherwise, she was dressed as usual – anything too obviously sexy might have given the game away. She explained to the pickets that she knew the strike could go on for weeks. She was happy about that: she supported the strikers. But during the strike, her two small children had gone to the country to stay with their grandmother. While they were away, she couldn't bear the thought of being without the photos of her kids she had on her desk. A secretary less pretty, in a skirt less short, might not have got away with it. But she did: the pickets smiled at her, let her in. She then collected, not the photos of her kids, but the packaging artwork.

I warned you that the exploited sex in this story was men not women – how pathetically vulnerable us blokes are to an attractive woman and a flattering smile.

Once Tom had the artwork, the rest was easy. He did not know how long the strike would run for, but he did know he'd be ready the second it was over.

He sent the packaging artwork to Italy and started printing packaging as fast as possible. He then sent the packs to P&G's Italian factory, and put them on generous overtime to manufacture and pack as much of P&G's main brand as they could.

In the meantime, he found and rented several big warehouses on the Italian side of the French/Italian border, and he stockpiled a huge amount of product – with French packaging – in the Italian warehouses. Finally, he rented a large fleet of trucks.

The strike ran for many weeks. During that time Tom's Italian warehouses started to bulge with product. The moment the strike was over, Tom's fleet of trucks rumbled over the border into France with massive supplies of soap.

Of course, every French supermarket had been starved of stuff to sell since the strike began. Once the P&G trucks were at their door they took all the product they could lay their hands on. P&G filled all the supermarket shelf space they normally had; but they also got most of Unilever's shelf space, as there wasn't any Unilever product to fill it. P&G's sales shot up; and Unilever lost a big chunk of market share that would take years to recover.

What is the moral of the story?

I think that there is not one moral, but three:

First, however intractable a problem seems, there's always an answer somewhere if you look hard and with a bit of imagination.

Second, intellectual cleverness isn't worth a light alongside pragmatic cleverness.

Third, if you're a mere man, standing in the picket line of a national strike, and a pretty woman with a rather short skirt comes up to you, please try not to be quite as gullible as those Frenchmen . . .

A magnum of thanks to ...

Jac, and Stephen, and Zoe, and Ceara, and both Davids, and Tim.

You made it possible, and you made it fun.

Index

Note: page numbers in **bold** refer to photographs.